Benedicta Leigh was b
working as a VAD du
trained at the Royal Ac
since performed widely
written most of her life,
She has two grown-up

In this remarkable autobiography, Benedicta Leigh por-
trays with painterly skill her insouciant, untrammelled
childhood and her troubled adult years. Using language
with wonderful freshness and originality, hers is a
unique voice, full of beauty, longing, pain and courage.

THE CATCH OF HANDS

AN AUTOBIOGRAPHY

BENEDICTA LEIGH

VIRAGO

Very many thanks to Virago, and particularly Amanda, for their kindness and patience in helping me to find myself again

Published by Virago Press Limited 1991
20–23 Mandela Street, Camden Town, London NW1 0HQ

*A CIP catalogue record for this book is
available from the British Library*

Printed in Great Britain by
Cox & Wyman Ltd, Reading, Berkshire

To Marigold Charlesworth, Diana Eden, John Smith
and my children, Sarah and Tom Vernon

T he bullet bit into my forehead as I skidded across the lawn and crashed to the ground. The decks ran crimson, and away by the hedge my mother slowly hauled up a great dandelion, its acrid milk spattering her knuckles. She was too busy to notice the rattle in my throat, my dying, my death, oh, the perfection of it, and she missed Ned the cabin boy weeping over my body and saying: 'O Captain, Sir, what will we do? Mr Peyton is dead and done for, and who shall drive the boat now?' 'Well, not him, anyway,' said Captain Tollemache. 'Get a coffin and some flags, and we will have a long, dull funeral and a party with ginger-beer. Everyone can come but Nanny, and my caterpillars will do an entertainment.'

I heard the boys whining and thumping up in the nursery as I turned over on to my stomach. My mother had gone indoors, leaving her straw hat on the steps, and spikes of grass bent beneath the anxiety of a beetle's progress. Over my shoulder blades a concentration of heat spilled, and the dog of war walloped towards me and leaned against my shoulder, a raggle of tongue pushing into my ear.

I said, 'You're being rather intimate with me today, my dear,' as I stroked him. His coat felt like a hot flannel. I sang: 'O dog of war, who forged thy dread breath?' And I sang that if it was stew for lunch, then I would be sick unto my plate a great lot. I sang a prayer that I could have more than half-a-crown for the fair, and that some people I knew had five shillings without even asking for it. And I sang: 'Grant Thou this thing, for I am the brightest and best of the morning. Amen.'

In the hall I aimed a punishing blow at my father's left flank, from which he would not recover in a hurry.

'Fall to your knees, you rat,' I said. I took my pistol out of my shorts pocket, put a cap in it and banged it, watching with satisfaction as he jumped elaborately and rolled over.

'Howl, you cur,' I said through gritted teeth. 'Howl, skunk.'

He howled: 'But I'm older than you. I'm just a poor old ragged downtrodden aged parent trying to keep my eldest unmarried daughter in comfort until I'm taken to the workhouse. What are you after?'

'I want long hair, oh please ask Mummy if I can, I mean supposing I'm asked to open the fête, how can I with short old stupid hair and a tortoiseshell slide and all these eyebrows?'

My father said: 'Wait until you're seventeen and Coming Out and doing the season. You'll be surprised at what happens then.'

I said: 'But supposing I'm suddenly asked to be a lion-tamer, I need to look like Shirley Temple, but with long hair and little embroidered frocks, not horrible party shoes and a vest, like little ratty dumb wet staggery disgusting babies wear? And how can I be beautiful with all these eyebrows spoiling my face?'

From the kitchen bulged the tallowy smell of Irish

stew, and my stomach side-stepped. I knew Mrs Paxford wasn't cooking it for the grown-ups.

My father and I sat on the last step of the stairs and he said: 'Do you think the whole world will open out for you if you are beautiful?'

I spat on one of the banisters, rubbed it with the heel of my hand, and said: 'Surely it's possible, provided Nanny and David don't stand in my way. But I shall need your best prayers, Daddy, all through the day and even when you're asleep.'

My father said: 'You know you've got them, and my love and my time for as long as you need them, and whether you're beautiful or not.'

He kissed me, and I touched the little dent on his forehead that he had from hanging on the barbed wire during the Great War. Twenty-four hours, they told him. No wonder it still hurt if you weren't careful.

I said: 'I want to ask you a serious question. Other people's smells apart, what do you think is the absolutely worst thing in the world?'

He didn't have to think, and I'd heard it before. He said: 'People who are only interested in themselves, only talk about themselves and only do what they want. There are four phrases unfailingly used by such people. One is, "We only go to the best places", the next is, "Only the best is good enough for me", the next is, "You know me", and the last, 'I know you".'

I have always known what he meant – the betrayal of a substandard spirit – shallow, vulgar and offensive.

A shift at the edge of my thoughts reminded me of something, and I said: 'I need to tell you about the going-away feeling I get sometimes. I told you before and I told John, but it isn't something I can understand and I think I have to tell you again.'

My father said: 'Tell me,' and I said: 'It's a sort of going away from myself, and I can see me very tiny and far-off, as though I don't really belong anywhere. Sometimes I'm afraid I won't be able to come back. I don't like that feeling. Do you know what it means?'

He said: 'No I don't really, but I think it's something quite a lot of people experience. On the whole, people are a bit frightened by such things and I think it's best not to talk about it too much, or perhaps only to me or Mummy – she would understand perfectly. Don't worry, though. Have you thought what you would like for your birthday?'

'No chance of an elephant, I suppose?' I said. 'No, all right then, how about a dagger and a frock with embroidery? Or could I be turned into a dog?'

'Certainly,' said my father. 'I will turn you into a dog wearing an embroidered frock and carrying a dagger between its teeth.'

I barked and jumped up at him, and he barked back over his shoulder as he went into the drawing room.

With considerable expertise I chased my tail for a moment. And went upstairs to the nursery for lunch, washing my hands on the way. A soggy bit of paper fell out of the tap, bearing the words: 'You'd better mind your manners, Madam.' A threat from the boys. I looked in the glass to see if I had curly hair, but I hadn't.

'I'm afraid I can't possibly eat this – it looks like plops,' I said pleasantly, settling into my chair.

'That'll do,' said Nanny.

I said: 'But it's horrible. You wouldn't even give it to a rhinoceros.'

John said: 'I would – I would – I would – I would.'

'You know what you'll get in a minute,' said Nanny.

'Yes-yes-yes-yes-yes,' said John.

'I feel rather not well,' I said faintly, leaning back in my chair. 'I'm afraid my eyes have got stuck up into my forehead again – no, don't touch me – the pain is terrible, but I will bear it until the doctor arrives . . .'

'Stop that rubbish and get on with your food, for goodness' sake,' snapped Nanny.

I thought, die. If I had golden ringlets and red patent-leather shoes and money, you wouldn't dare. I ate a mouthful and said to John: 'The dog of war is going to be my dressing-room dog when I'm an actress, and when anyone knocks at my door, he will thrang them away.'

'Thrang?' said John.

'Yes. Sort of push. You know,' I said.

'Pushing's no good, he'd have to jump up at their frotes.'

'He's a bit short for that,' I said.

John said: 'We could stretch him. Put him upside down and pull his legs upwards. And we could take turns,' he added kindly.

I said: 'He wouldn't look so sweet stretched, and his ears would be too sort of high off the ground.'

We looked down at the dog of war, his eyes molten with remembered lechery, and I squeaked him a bit of potato.

John said: 'We could paint his ears to look nearer the ground. Or stick stuff on to them.'

'What stuff?' I said, and when he said, 'Plasticine', I yelped, 'Plasticine ears? On our dog of war? The other dogs would laugh.'

My brother spat a piece of gristle on to his plate, and Nanny drew in a breath, but said nothing, let it go, the weather being warm and her off to Hove the next day.

5

She did not care for John's intrepidity nor for my lack of curly hair.

I considered the dog of war's ears, and said: 'He'd eat the Plasticine, anyway – sort of snap quickly back over his shoulder and eat it, like this—.' I snapped quickly back over my shoulder and growled.

'All right then, what about Meccano?' said John.

'Meccano!' I shouted. 'You can't – just think of the screws going in, it would hurt, and it would rattle, he'd have rattling ears – we couldn't do that.'

The pudding was stewed apples. The apples had not been cored properly, so there were toenails in it. I picked mine out and put them round the edges of my plate. 'Five,' I said. 'Sweet little toenail children. I love you.' I rubbed my forehead, the feeling of genuine illness beginning to snatch at me.

'If I am well enough,' I said to John, 'you may come and watch one of my latest deaths after rest, where I get bitten by a tiger in Meerut. Lots of blood.'

He said, 'No,' and I said, 'Oh go on, you can be Daddy's bearer, Hafiz Kamahan Sultan Khan, oh do . . .'

'No,' said John.

But, lying on my bed after lunch, I recognised the dry fronds of malaise licking at my temples. Illness dominated my childhood and though my parents were familiar with it, I felt my wretchedness would not be welcome so soon after their return from India. I was never fussed over, but since I had once nearly died, my ailments claimed an extra canopy of care, and now became swaddled in the murmurous safety of the sick-room. The routine, early set in my life, was repeated regularly, with the same love and vigilance and with

small disturbance to the household. My mother's cracking beauty and gifted nursing gentled me well again,
without effort, though my eventual emergence from
bed each time showed just as gingerly. Until then, my
head supported like an infant, I took from a white
invalid cup, beef tea, or sometimes arrowroot laced
with brandy, both as pleasant and sustaining as such
delicacies have been for centuries.

My mother abandoned a great deal to be with me,
sometimes reading aloud, with flair, sometimes merely
lying on the sofa – but whether I tossed beneath a
clammy mosquito net in Malta or groaned in England's
winter, she seldom left me. One breathless Maltese
afternoon only was I left with the servants, and the
sandal-flap and giggle from the kitchen advised me of
protection in the hot stillness.

*Someone is there, the darkness stealing over him. My fear is
immediate and the sound I make is seized and strung and kept
mute for all my lagging days. And I am changed.*

I had not learned to fear doctors in my childhood, and
Dr Hunter-Dunn, having delivered me, knew my con-
stitution and loved children. By his instruction the
chemist rendered nasty medicine pleasant by way of
raspberry cordial, and thus were remedial properties
encouraged, and younger patients both pleased and
restored.

Dr Hunter-Dunn's goodness blazed from him, his
vigorous yet gentle talent proclaiming an absolute vocation. Without apparent interest he would mark my
breathing, my colour and my pulse; then without the
raillery or archness employed by some doctors with

young people, he listened to the stories I had written. Intently. Charmingly.

He, then, my bondsman, I was his for these addresses, and fondly we noted one another, he with *dégagé* expertise, I with odious confidence that my scrutiny was not being rumbled.

Custom having made of me a docile patient, I soon remarked the promise of convalescence glimmering a near cry away, and, school happily disallowed, began to reap the gains of my seclusion, emerging, I felt certain, the more valued, greatly interesting and unquestionably paler. As usual, the fulfilment of this promise stood only upon the degree of excitement I was considered able to sustain, and cloudily in the world once more, my first rapture was the tumultuous joy of reunion with my white mice. Less taxing, though still rewarding, was a *rapprochement* with the dog of war, to whom absolution was freely granted for having peed outside my sickroom door.

Made powerful by a little spoiling, I spent much time ordering richly from *Ellisdon's Joke Catalogue*, bossed my brothers about a good deal, and sometimes recumbent, occasionally in a wheelchair, I read and read and wrote and wrote and wrote, sustained by little delicate meals, designed to remedy a thinness.

I noticed something about myself early in my life. Something not rare, sometimes useful, and over which I had no control – the complete absorption into my memory of all experiences and situations of importance – locked until released. Then I could play them back in my consciousness, sharp and clear as when they were first captured by recall, the turntable that pulls us round and round, shrieking the same excuses, tangling the same skeins, wailing the same old prayers. And from the muttering reaches of contingency, the stockpile winds and stretches and pulls, the hash settling only at my life's contracted end.

O turn me into Shirley Temple with all those presents, I besought day and night, my dreams singed with envy. And let my shadow freewheel into yours, Tom Mix, with that most whopping charm, and a bonus horse as well, the range at our beck while the world lasts. I may seem like Shirley Temple, but I am better at looking after people. Stay with me, Mr Mix, and I will never let you be hurt or die, even when the people leave the cinema and go out into the rain. You can trust me, Tom. Let the nursery burn with golden guineas, and I will buy fame in Hollywood and be your guardian. I must have pink frocks, frills, curly hair and embroidery, but it is also necessary for me to be in the saddle when the bugle sounds. Twopence a week is laughable for me – I need proper money, and carving angels for my brothers' miniature cemetery in the garden earns neither spondulicks nor gratitude.

There may be something in Daddy's library about instantaneous and abundant money-minting. No, so a quick read of the old favourites – *Dodsworth, Thunder on the Left, Hudson River Bracketed* and, saved till the last, *The Erotic History of France* – always interesting, not least for the fastidiousness of its language.

Tease out from me the fluff and the scramble and leave me a bright, clear life, great with coin. Because, Mummy, twopence a week is really not enough, and you must know that. I can't ask, I'm too well brought up, and you know that too. I need the money for training caterpillars. I have to build them a big top, surely I told you about that, apart from having to be Shirley Temple. It all costs money, you know.

If richness were already attained, I would settle my parents in a small but charming cottage at my gates. Nanny would be pensioned off but shown magnanimity, and my brothers would be allowed to stay, and be grateful. I would go into the kitchen like my mother, to see the cook, and say: 'Hallo. We will have anchovy eggs and trifle for lunch. And get some ginger-beer. My brothers will have water, they are too young for ginger-beer. I will have Joker to sleep on my bed, but he must be bathed because he has been a smelly dog for weeks, and I shall be wearing a handmade pink nightdress with daisies. And ribbon. And it mustn't smell of Joker. We will have a party tomorrow, and there must be ice cream and sausages. Also a cake with hundreds and thousands. I am going out now to buy a few kittens. Goodbye.'

How natural, yet loathsome, are the flamboyance and discourtesy that so often attend the acquisition of riches. Would not my parents have set upon me for such lack of politeness and breeding? Indeed so, had they not been out soliciting in the streets, clad in designer rags.

Tom Mix, give us a ride of your horse and a hold of your hand, my life's end reaching away until I tumble to it, and come with me, with me, come with me, and I'll look back at you. Cactus and Cherokee, a hundred head of cattle, oh Tom, the squeak of leather, the crack of my gun, I will cook for you and bind up your bullet wounds. I don't marry people, but give us a lend of your horse, and I will gentle you both as long as we shall live.

Under the oak tree in the garden, I wept for the starlit

prairie and my steadfastness, and dreamed of money to get me to Arizona wearing a Shirley Temple frock embroidered with ducks.

Through the grille at the bank, I burned and hissed at the cashier like St Elmo's Fire, saying, 'Oh please, only two and six, that's all, just to get me to Tom Mix who has invited me to be his good and faithful dog forever, you always let my mother have some, oh, go on, please.' I barked softly and cracked my forehead on the counter, and blood threaded thinly, darkly, down my face, the face of an intrepid dog who would save people from floods.

My mother, there as cover, clicked up to me, dispersed the audience, sighed despairingly and walked me out, saying, 'Please don't do that again, darling.'

I walked beside her on all fours with my tongue hanging out, stopping occasionally for a luxury scratch in the cello position. 'I am Spot of Arizona,' I whined. 'You must stroke me and scrunch my ears about, and call me Spot.'

She said: 'Come on darling, please,' and I jumped up at her and said: 'You didn't call me Spot.' She said, 'Spot', in a low, embarrassed voice, and I licked her hand convulsively and said, 'Tread on my paw, so that I can squeak.' I threatened to have a pee at the next lamppost if she didn't.

'By all means do,' she said. 'I do not imagine the sight of a small girl using a lamppost as a lavatory will cause much of a brouhaha.' I squeaked anyway, and got up and jumped about tremendously, sideways, and fell down. I excelled in biting the dust, from commonplace purlers to occasion-wreckers such as coming a cropper down the cathedral steps as a two-year-old bridesmaid

11

at my aunt's wedding. Shown on newsreels throughout the country.

The screaming pumps out of me, and through the spy-hole they watch my life change.

'The labourer is worthy of his hire,' said my mother as she gave me the pocket money I had earned by weeding the drive. At the post office I bought a twist of aniseed balls, each tenderly pinkish, touchingly brown, and each begot with a hated caraway seed that wretchedly impaired the climactic bite.

At breakfast, staying with cousins, pocket money was whisked to each child on a lazy Susan, and the nodding warmth of the dining room was quickened by this weekly allocation of spondulicks. As a mere guest I expected nothing, and for sensibility's sake scrutinised the dog, who, possessed, jumped up at my knees and embedded his claws in the skin. My clean cotton frock bore several small holes, and the traces of blood. Since he was not our dog of war, I could do nothing, and when the lazy Susan stopped in front of me blazing with two whole shillings instead of my accustomed two-pence, I was pale and bowed with gratitude, and forgave him. 'Thank you,' I said. 'Thank you very much.' And I marvelled.

Each having discharged our morning obligations, we issued from neat bedrooms, hair brushed, pocket money put by, the garden awaiting us, already blanched and listless from the morning heat.

Always awkward with each other initially, yet we felt dandled by the prospect of some really thunderous dissipation, and spoke sweetly for the first day, our voices limpid and courteous. That morning, we walked through the long grasses, and to show our ease with each other sometimes sprang and capered like tumblers until the heat began to pick our spirits clean. Then we fell against each other and lay shifting and pulsating as amiably as a farrow of little pigs, and as fragrantly.

Mornings and occasional afternoons were spent in a straw teepee, having discussions. We sat in a circle on the ground, our chins on our knees, our feet a dusty thicket in the centre. For me the very cone shape seemed to have the signature of intrigue, and I felt daring and intelligent, and hoped something would be asked of me, but it was not, for my insufferable zeal generally deterred the most indulgent.

There was a restless, yeasty quality in the teepee, as though some essence worked in the straw, fetching a steamy warmth through its walls that smelt as close and familiar as my own identity. I liked it and snuffed it up happily, burying my nose in the crook of my elbow. It smelt like I did, protective and enduring, and belonging only to myself. It was part of the matrix that I would never quite shed. Small cusps of light pierced the straw here and there, and jigged about the floor.

That morning we did not start talking immediately, but sat quietly. A smudge of insects shuddered above us in the air and sweat pressed our clothes to us like paint. When the talking began, it was about having babies and that kind of thing, and I did not join in because I did not like talking to kin about such things. Also, I did not wish to reveal how little I knew about the subject. So I took out my penknife and some paper which I cut into fierce little squares, and sometimes I made militant gestures with my knife. I did this because we were to ride after lunch, and riding with other people still put quite a lot of wind up me, unless I knew them well.

Standing beside the horse I was to ride that afternoon, I trembled. Prodigious, it massed over me like a canopy, and I seemed to stand beneath its gentle belly. Yet it was not so big, nor I so small, but simply that I was accustomed to a little pony. I said: 'I'm not really used to anything quite this bigness.' But a kind of doggedness took my scruff as I mounted. A cousin shouted, 'You'll be all right,' and I shouted back, 'Of course I will.'

And the sunny afternoon was suddenly and roughly taken, the sky crowding and darkening. A paw of wind swiped at me, and I moaned and swallowed. I hope someone's going to be proud of me, I thought. We had broken into a canter, and the fields were licking away in front of us and sluicing away each side like water. I could not see the others and became small with fear as the gallop seized us. My thoughts were flattened and I was in the thick of my own fright as I realised that the others had vanished and that we were runaways, that great elemental horse and I. Obliviously, we jumped a farm gate and began to slow down as the rain started. After a bit the cousins came up rather white-faced to see if I was all right. Quietly, we went home and I felt sick with relief, dismounting rather showily and walking into the house with the slightest swagger.

In the vicarage garden we rehearsed the maypole dance all the morning. And in my chest burst a furious lament that I was cast as a boy dancer and not a girl.

The girls, I noted, kicking one of the vicar's geraniums, wore flowered sunbonnets and petticoats with lace insertion. The boys, of which I was one, wore thick, bunched ploughboy's smocks made of holland.

14

And the morning was as hot as ginger and as dry and thirsty as the end of the world. My hair stuck to my nape and I muttered, 'Take me to Thy bosom, Lord, I am Thy servant. Next time there is a fête, see that I am a girl, or I will crack the sky down upon Miss Johnson's head and her pointy little feet also, and it will be a pleasure. Let me be a girl next fête day, Lord, and let me wear a frock with embroidery on it and a flowered sunbonnet. And let there be ginger-beer at tea-time because I don't really like lemonade out of bottles.'

In the vicarage garden, which was next to ours, Miss Johnson was cross with us for tangling the ribbons of the maypole. 'When are we going to do it properly? When?' we cried, envisaging our glory, not really needing to ask, knowing it to be at tea-time, our parents smiling upon us as the girls pertly pranced and the boys lumbered. Round the pole the wide ribbons would perfectly lap and cross and plait, Miss Johnson out of sight counting for us, in her vee-necked blue with the picot edging.

But now was elevenses, with milk and Marie biscuits. There was Dundee cake under tissue paper on the stalls, and jaunty little jam tarts, crookedly decorated with blobs of Vienna icing. They were not for elevenses, but would be for sale in the afternoon, sold by ladies in shiny brown straw hats and with welcoming teeth, their dreadful bags on the grass under the stalls.

The year before, I had seen a Skye terrier pee on one of the bags, and looked forward to it happening again. Drinking our milk, we wandered about, picking, stroking, choosing what we might later buy, after we had thumped round the maypole and Miss Johnson was wiping her neck with a chiffon scarf and being congratulated by our parents.

We sat on the vicar's lawn with biscuit crumbs in the creases of our knees, and I thought, I might buy that turquoise bead bag I saw on the white elephant stall. If I have the money. Which I might have after I have been home for lunch.

The vicar's dining room, where we changed for going home, was long and dark, with a mock Jacobean table and chairs with barley sugar legs, the stain worn at the turns. With hushed giggles we laid our maypole clothes on the table, and putting our own ones on, trooped out of the French windows and home.

It was fish pie, greens and stewed pears, and the nursery table was already laid. The boys were sitting waiting, David in a feeder, and I could see at once that Nanny was wishing I were some nice little girl like Shirley Rat Temple with ringlets.

'I fear I shall have to have mine at once,' I said in an *affairé* voice like my mother. Both the boys looked at me like who did I think I was. After lunch I said in my *affairé* voice that I was afraid I must leave at once, and had Mummy left me some spending money? She had, Nanny said, it was on the hall table, she was having her hair done, and would see me at the fête.

Two shillings. I was hoping it would be two shillings and sixpence, like I always had for the fair. The turquoise bead bag cost ninepence, which wouldn't leave much, and I usually bought something for my parents and a token of some kind for the dog. I would make certain of the bead bag before anything else. It might have been snapped up already, it was so pretty.

When I got back to the vicarage garden, I saw Canon Challacombe and his eyebrows eating a Shrewsbury biscuit by the greenhouse and smiling through the crumbs in a courtly way which rather disturbed me. But since I was a believer in God and retribution, I smiled back. After all, I liked him in spite of the courtliness. I went to the White Elephant stall to make sure my bead bag was still there. It was, and I turned it over and back, already in love with its imperfections – a bead missing, the clasp faulty, all forgiven for its colour and pliancy. There was also a spider made of black wool, with one of its legs gone. I picked it up and looked at it carefully, wondering if my mother would like it. She may have been looking for something like that for ages. You could hang it up by a black thread just behind its head. She might like to hang it somewhere in the drawing room. She hadn't anything else like that in there. 'My daughter gave it to me,' she would say.

I left the stall and went to fall on the grass with the others until the fête opened at two-thirty. Our maypole dance was not until four, which was tea-time, and Miss Johnson said we needn't dress up until three-thirty and that we could spend our money from two-thirty till then. Lying flat on the grass with my arms out like an aeroplane, I visualised Canon Challacombe slowly walking up the aisle completely naked, and with a long pale courtly wozzname, but I didn't laugh because I thought, well why not? Why shouldn't he?

I thought about the kind of figure I would cut at four o'clock, hatefully attired in a holland smock, a stupid boy's stupid hat on my stupid head, my chagrin watched by the whole of Farnborough including my stupid brothers and, oh dear, my parents. I hope you all die before four o'clock, I thought, except Mummy and Daddy.

Miss Johnson and the gramophone would be out of sight behind the bushes, and the music, 'In an English

Country Garden', would be faint and reedy, but unmistakable. Miss Johnson would wait until we were standing in our places, and would then declare in a resonant contralto: 'AND', which meant the music would start at any moment.

Suddenly it was two-thirty, and the fête was declared open, and affable greetings began to pucker through the gathering crowds. Tricked-out babies ruthlessly posseted over their mothers' shoulders, and the scouts managed the coconut shy, clean as picked apples, their caps slammed on stooks of bright hair.

I belted straight to the white elephant stall for my bead bag, and the woolly spider for my mother. I could see the spider at once, but I could not see the bead bag, and my hands began to stampede over the counter in awful panic. Tears squeezed out of my eyes, and the lady in charge said, 'Cheer up, dear, what about a nice notebook with an embroidered cover?' I gave a childish sob and shook my head. There was a knitted hat, a felt egg-cosy with a hen's head, and a Sunny Jim doll with sawdust seeping from one of his feet. Nothing else.

Suddenly, I saw it – I saw my bead bag. Like an iridescent fish it lay upon the counter, a great clumsy teapot standing upon its chaste elegance. My head swam and I almost fell on my knees with relief. Roughly I removed the horrid teapot, and gently picked up my bead bag, putting it against my cheek. O God, I whispered, Thou art utterly kind, and I am Thy Servant. Intemperate with gratitude, I paid for it ostentatiously, and raucously insisted upon a penny off the black woolly spider. With unaccustomed boldness I said that a spider with one leg missing was no good as a present to anyone. Every now and then I looked at and stroked my bead bag. When I had just seen it, before the fête was open, I had thought it pretty, but of no great account. It was when I had rushed up to the stall, and could not see it, rumpled the counter and could not find it, and then suddenly there it was lying so patient, so sweet, with that awful teapot on it – that was when my heart burst and I knew it was of my flesh, like in the Prayer Book, and that I must have it. Grateful and holy, I asked the lady for threepence off the Sunny Jim doll with a hole in its foot. She said no. It was, I said nauseatingly, for my two little brothers to share between them. She said I could mend it, so I said oh all right, and I bought my father some pins and a handkerchief with *Angela* embroidered on it.

I sat down on the grass with my booty, and opened the bead bag in case there was something in it, and there was. Inside was a kirby grip, and a round Tangée rouge box with a smudge of strawberry colour on a piece of cotton wool. And I knew at once that the bag was too beautiful, and that it was unworthy to give my mother the woolly spider, and to keep the bag for myself, yet I had to, and felt redeemed from the sin by the hell of having to dance round a maypole in front of all Hampshire dressed up as a ploughboy. 'Ransom'd, heal'd, restor'd, forgivern,' I sang quietly, and I also asked forgiveness for having thought about Canon Challacombe's wozzname, which I never meant to think of, it just came into my head. And I thought how nice it would be to be the actual Lamb of God, and for everyone to know you were, and call you it. Jumping about with hooves and sweet little ears. Better than a ploughboy.

The vicar's lawn had been cut the evening before, and now it smelt warm and safe, a bit like honey. Soon we must go into the house and change into our maypole

19

clothes, and then my parents would arrive, just as the tea-stall opened, my brothers with them in clean shorts and polished strap shoes. As we walked in to change for the maypole dance, Dr and Mrs Hunter-Dunn waved at me, and I to them. I did not then know that he had delivered me of my screaming mother, myself to scream for loss and sadness half my life.

I looked back at the maypole, sinless and Arcadian, spoiling for our brigandage, the ribbons falling from the top, straight and still, and with a powerful innocence.

My parents and the boys arrived in time for tea and rock cakes, leaving Nanny to have a nice lay-down at home. The afternoon sky had become opaque and dullish, and I loathsome in my ploughboy's smock, my eyebrows populating my whole face.

'Don't frown, darling,' said my mother.

'I'm trying to get the eyebrows away,' I said.

'They won't just go away,' she said. 'Wait until you've grown up, you'll like them then. They're Taylor eyebrows, like mine, rather handsome.'

I gave the Sunny Jim doll to my brothers to share. David was quite young so he started chewing it; and John pulled it away from him, and thwacked it against a tree, and kicked it all over the garden until my father took it away from him.

I took the spider out of my pocket and suddenly dangled it in front of my mother's face for a surprise, and she gasped and said: 'Goodness me!' and we all laughed. 'It's a present,' I said and she said it was lovely, and how clever I was. She meant it too. When I gave the embroidered *Angela* hankerchief to my father, he looked at it very carefully and admiringly, and didn't say any of those silly grown-up things that people say, and I stood shining up at them both, feeling proud. I leaned against my mother and said: 'Shall I show you what I got for myself? Do you want to see it?' And I took the bead bag and held it up in front of them, and they both said what good taste I had. I knew they'd like it.

Miss Rouse was coming towards us, wearing pink earrings, and my head began to fizz, and I swallowed. Oh please, oh my goodness me, why am I not wearing my party frock, instead of this old smock? Miss Rouse, please say something to me, oh please.

She spoke to my parents, and, lightly putting a hand on my shoulder, said: 'Isn't she growing up quickly?' but she didn't seem to mean it. Not really.

'Are you all enjoying yourselves?' she said, smiling. She closed her lips softly between each word. It was formidable.

If only she'd said I was beautiful, and closed her lips like that. But she hadn't, and I could see Miss Johnson's little pointy shoes running about collecting us children for the maypole dance. The talking softened and stopped and people began to arrange themselves to watch us – in their hands Mrs Kinsley's rock cakes, better than ever this year. The sky had become oyster-coloured, and a drop of rain splashed on to my temple. I heard Miss Johnson calling, 'Come along, children, before it rains,' as the drops quickened a little. I walked up to my place and took the end of my ribbon, feeling with pleasure the cool fingerprints of rain, and I heard Miss Johnson say, 'AND'.

The music started thinly from behind the bushes, and each smiling, each pointing our right toe, we danced, and I turned my head and felt that I was flying, and that there was no sound. And I thought, my life will begin when I am ready for it. When I am ready for it, then my life will begin. It will be different, I shall be I, someone will love and understand me. I shall be I, and you shall be you. Struggles recaptured years later with such immaculate pain and force.

It rained, and I ran almost all the way home, feeling very light, as though I had no substance – I was trounced by the rain. I jumped down the little grassy bank at the side of the house and did a somersault and sat with my face turned upwards to catch the drops in my mouth, and I thought, I am I. Whatever happens to me I will always be I. The rain came down in a sudden heavy rush, and the others ran past me and into the house.

'Wait!' I shouted. 'I have to tell you all something – I feel – I feel all sort of different. As if something were going to happen – oh, listen – can't you wait?'

But they had gone, and, soaked and elated, I went indoors and up to the nursery bathroom where I could hear David's bath running already, and his and Nanny's warring voices picked at my ears like a cat's claw.

On Filey beach, my thoughts pulled for home and my caterpillar and the dog of war. The teasing sea grappled the beach, flying towards us, and the whole litter of children squeaked and scampered away from it. Filey cousins and Filey aunts took care of part of our summer holidays. The aunts, unmarried but familiar with Truby King, were fond of children and often said so. Sometimes asked to family parties, where they wore cairngorm brooches and amber bracelets, their intrusive brio embarrassed us greatly. Since they spoke mainly through the use of little saws and adages, the day was wrung dry of communication before we had even finished breakfast, and any further verbal exchanges were merely arid first drafts, too infertile to bear.

Sometimes, sitting on their deck chairs, the aunts looked troubled, as though they had failed some examination that was simple enough for them to have passed without exertion. They were kind, but in their eyes was a cancelled look, which worried and depressed me. They were not fortunate in their choice of Macclesfield silk blouses, and in general had an over-grazed appearance with rather vanquished-looking cleavages covered in splashy freckles.

That afternoon, with the sun low on Filey beach and our skins prickling from salt and the hot day that still hung over us, it was time to go back to the house for tea. Vibrant and dedicated, the aunts put away their books, collected striped bathing suits and cardigans, and picked us off the sands one by one like nuts. First, standing and shading their eyes, they would call us in like authoritative birds and then grasp our hands in a forceful compelling way, which we liked, and bear us off. One of them bent over me, revealing, apart from the freckles, a pink lock-knit petticoat which made me feel rather squeamish, and brought within range the entire question of what kind of underclothes aunts wore, and the possibility of knickers being open to scrutiny in the near future. My friends and I took an interest in knickers, and discussions and comparisons were *de rigueur*, generally taking place in someone's shrubbery or potting shed.

At Filey Vicarage we sat down to tea, rinded of our salty sunsuits, the butter melting on neat slices of bread, cut with a hot knife in the kitchen.

The milk in our glasses had turned slightly and familiarly, since domestic refrigerators were rare. We were not at home, and consequently behaved in a constrained and civilised manner, neither smacking our lips nor catching each other's eyes and giggling. Because it was a holiday, the aunts had kindly ordered Playbox Biscuits with their strident-coloured icing so wonderfully brittle and alluring. We ate them with polite deliberation, deftly skimming vulgar crumbs from round our mouths with reptilian tongues. Looking out of the window, I wished for home. This homesickness assailed me every time I went away, pushing open my stomach with the wheel and turn of a flock of birds, until I got back to the warm smell of my own covert, and the shape of my life already minted, and without uncertainties.

I know, I know you, I saw you, saw your fist in the bleeding of me, in my life. I will always see you.

Aunt Maud was different from the other Filey aunts, as slight as a spindle and older. Up from her forehead mantled a brisk engaging foam of white hair, and we were charmed by her childlike spirits, pressing for her favours with rash impatience denied the other aunts.

For this cherished Edwardian aunt, who wore a black velvet choker and pince-nez, was not only our friend and confidante but the loving pianist for our dancing after tea. Bunched up at one end of the room, as ridiculous as young dogs, we waited for the opening chords of 'Sir Roger de Coverley' and watched the late sun streak Aunt Maud's shoulder and her appealing head. A wide scarf of seaweed stirred and plucked at the window frame with a pagan innocence, foretelling the weather for us, and Aunt Maud turned and smiled, adjusting her pince-nez. The roughhouse that ensued as she touched the keyboard was exactly what we looked forward to and she encouraged us. 'Goodness gracious,

I thought the house was coming down!' she would say, and you knew she would hardly care if it did, as we stampeded up and down the room, breathless and scarlet. 'It's like a herd of buffalo!' she crowed joyfully, watching the turmoil with a practised eye, for she knew precisely when the curtain must come down, and that a little turbulence before bedtime was beneficial for the young. And so, the ultimate abandonment of the polka, the heady rhythmic stamping that inevitably ended in a resonant collision, boys stamping on girls with sharp victorious cries, girls tumbling to the ground in pettish mounds. 'Now look what you've done!' they would pipe waspishly, retrieving slides and hair ribbons from the floor, chastely smoothing frocks over guiltless loins, swearing, and I with them, that boys were beastly and that marriage must be horrid. Softly and predictably, Aunt Maud smiled. For at that time marriage was considered the only way in which to be fulfilled and happy. And, smiling at us, she let her hands drop easily to her lap.

In the potting shed some weeks later, my friend, mindful of my education, disclosed the information that marriage was directly related to being bare, and that you couldn't get married unless you were prepared to be bare quite a lot of the time.

I was, of course, perfectly astonished by this intelligence, and somewhat disturbed. I was certain that nothing of the kind ever happened in our household, except when one occupied the bathroom, and even then the grown-ups locked the door.

My friend looked at me and I looked back at her.

'Bare?' I said. 'Why?'

She said that sometimes both of you had to be bare.

'You mean sitting having lunch, both bare?' I said. 'But supposing one of the dogs came in?'

She said: 'Dogs wouldn't notice, they're bare all the time. Anyway, it's mostly in the bedroom people do it.'

'Do what?' I said, and she whispered in my ear. My voice seemed absconded when it came out. I said: 'Are you sure? I mean what's the point of that? It sounds disgusting. I'm not going to let anyone do that to me, I can tell you.'

She shrugged, and I recklessly tore a scab off my knee which bled quite a lot, and I felt better. But it all sounded peculiar, and we didn't look at each other. My father's batman, Nunn, had taught me to snap my fingers, so I did some of that.

'Stop it!' she whispered. She was a bit older than me and had curly hair. Suddenly, I felt unsure that I really liked her, but I wanted to ask her something more. So I asked her what happened after people had finished doing it.

She said: 'They have cigarettes. Sometimes they have drinks as well.'

'Then what?' I said.

She looked at me and said: 'I think they sometimes do it again. So it must be quite nice. Probably.'

'Are they bare all this time?' I said.

She said: 'Well, of course, silly. They couldn't do it otherwise, could they?'

I didn't answer. Somehow, she made me feel uneasy, indeed most wretchedly discomposed. But, nonetheless, there was one more significant question I needed to ask.

'How do you know all this?' I asked.

'They left the door open once,' she said.

I said: 'I'm going to talk to Nunn in the stables. He's going to make me a peg doll and he's teaching me to whistle. I'm afraid you can't stay to tea because there are only four chocolate biscuits and I'm going to have two and the dog of war will have the other two. So you can go home now,' I said. It was a lie. The dog of war was never allowed chocolate biscuits and I only had them for treats. I wanted her to get out of the shed, out of our territory and if practical, out of the country. Because I felt she shouldn't have watched. I didn't go to the stables, because I felt a bit odd and shaky. I went indoors and gave the dog of war a long, comforting fussy stroke which hushed my sudden insecurity.

My mind felt stripped and untenanted, presenting only a tundra implanted with awkward and unwelcome facts I could not accept. So I kicked a few stones about, before visiting my sick bat in the outhouse. The boys were out, and I did not wish to see my mother after what I had discovered, so I trailed up into the nursery where Nanny sat knitting and wearing her customary redoubtable black hat. Both of us controlled expressions of aversion at the sight of each other. She had long given me up as possible wunderkind material, instead choosing to groom my youngest brother for stardom. A necessary fury flooded me as I went in and I wanted to be enclosed and nested, and to feel safe. But oh, then I knew I must allow it and embrace it and that my life would pull away ahead of me, and I would become its shift and settle, whatever the drubbing I gave it.

I walked up to Nanny and stroked her arm in the tight, white cotton blouse with the eyelet embroidery, and she went on knitting, but with a scrap of a smile that dressed my rawness.

'I feel a bit sort of pain-y,' I said, although rallying somewhat.

'Don't be silly,' said Nanny. 'Settle down and do

some crayoning. You been picking in the kitchen garden again? Serve you right if you've got worms.'

I retched ostentatiously, and she went on knitting. I thought, I bet you don't know what I know.

But as I thought it, my stomach began to list a bit, and I could not retain what I had been told.

'Oh Nanny,' I wailed suddenly, and butted her. 'I feel funny. I don't feel safe. I want to be someone else.' I felt my face the mask of furious childhood, but for once Nanny Farnell was well inclined.

'Growing pains, I shouldn't wonder,' she said. 'Like a fruit drop?' She took one from the treat jar and shoved it in my mouth, adding, 'What do you say?' So I said it of course. 'Thank you, Nanny.'

'Who is it you want to be, duck?' she said.

'Tom Mix and his horse,' I said.

'Both of them?' said Nanny.

I said: 'Yes. Then you've got both of them for friends.'

'Wouldn't you rather be Princess Margaret Rose? She's a dainty little thing,' she said.

'No thanks,' I said. Nanny's pink wool fell on the floor, and I picked it up in my teeth and offered it to her. She took it and remembered to call me Spot, and I felt better. I said I could see her knickers, and she said that wasn't very nice, was it? I said I was sorry, and the feeling of wanting to be someone else began tunnelling about inside me.

Sitting under the table, I said, 'If I were two people, we could read to each other. And if I were just one different person, like Shirley Temple, I wouldn't be here at all.'

'Pigs', said Nanny, 'could fly.'

Things were easy, and already familiar. In my head

was a spatter of thoughts still, but now I felt comfortable about things, almost as though they had always been a part of me.

'Go and comb your hair, duck,' said Nanny, 'and wash your face. You look like a sweep.'

So, for a while, Nanny and I were friends and sat together with a contained irritation that was almost harmony, until my youngest brother staggered in and fell down and screamed and was picked up and fussed over. But today I didn't mind, because I felt different, so I went outside and into the kitchen garden and crammed raspberries into my mouth, and padded about in the soft dusty evening. Inside me was fetched a little seed of sweetness which was almost pain, and though I felt it was a usual thing I'd learned, yet I needed healing all the same.

I thought about my parents, a thread pulling us one to the other, supple and moderate, everything different now, and felt a swanky fondness for them, as though they were my children now, and I their parent. I said Amen to that day, but felt I had a fragile importance.

A jostle of tobacco flowers pushed round the residentiary at Chichester, where my grandfather was archdeacon, and where we sometimes stayed. The scent buffeted through the open windows of his study every evening, and we had had Mrs Allwood's trifle for lunch. The garden and the little fountain shimmered and we played with boats and snapdragon heads, our voices thinned from heat and good behaviour.

When she was in her twenties, my grandmother, wearing white and holding a violin, was painted by Sir John Collier. A proclaimed Edwardian beauty already, the portrait hung in the Fair Women Exhibition at the

Grafton Gallery. Yet there was something about her that was still unfixed and undecided.

With careless vanity, she once said that no one ever liked it anyway – that Americans or Martians might perhaps buy it for vast sums in future generations, but no more than that.

It has not been sold yet.

In middle age, she was beautiful and redoubtable. She was also amusing, intelligent and fastidious, and people of all ages fell in love with her. She was a romantic, with a distaste for sentimentality, as I have, and a loathing for trappings and pretensions. She bullied, threatened and adored my grandfather, who found it greatly to his liking, and laughed a good deal. I never saw two people so love each other, except my parents, perhaps.

Her letters to me began with dignity and affection, and she was one of my earliest preceptresses, causing me trepidation and joy.

'Dearest Child,' she would write. The sheets of paper were large, thick and flax-coloured, and the writing defined and resolute. She had a gift for phrasing and vocabulary, and her punctuation was valid and incisive. It became important to go nowhere without pencil and paper, since a mental tally was not greatly reliable, and an exorbitantly memorised plate of eggs and bacon could expunge everything else. Except praise, generally remembered word for word with indecent clarity, and for many years.

In the pool in the Chichester garden, the goldfish hung, turning a little, the water moving. They were bright and then dark and when I put my hand in it, they churned away and down like falling coins.

Round the corner of the house was the other pool,

with the chipper little fountain firing a frail, sporadic fusillade, damping our hair and clothes, and us loving it and trying to fall in. The holly tree was a strapping giant, tall enough to benight the catchpenny fish in the pond when the sun was ruined and gone in the afternoon. You could go inside it, right inside, and I took dressing-up robes for being a bishop and pencils for candles. Under the prickly skirts of the holly tree, I held lengthy ritualistic church services, for I believed in God and in virtue, and I was good and timid – much too timid to be anything else but good.

But I had one wickedness. In my grandparents' great and worshipful bathroom, where everything smelt grown up, and the towels were like fleeces, I used to sit in my bath and have a clandestine suck of my sponge. And next morning at family prayers, I bent the knee and begged forgiveness, the smell of our breakfast, smoked haddock, coming through the green baize door, Mrs Allwood accompanying it in a spray of hairpins, as we all assembled in the hall for prayers.

After Mrs Allwood, Patty came in, angular, moderate and gentle, who unpacked your trunk for you, and always brought the early morning tea. Collings was next, slightly ruffled from Grandmother's affectionate teasing, predicted rather than realised. Collings always had the wretched expression of a wrong-doer, and made tremulous dashes to and from the dining room while waiting at lunch, as though the law were after her. Violet, the kitchen maid, who came in last of all, seldom left the haven of the kitchen, suffering pangs of awkwardness if we met, pared to the bone with shyness and dumb with confusion. Though I wonder if she may not have been quite a droll upon her own ground, amongst the Christmas cracker jokes, with a glass of reasonable port in her hand. Or perhaps Violet was always somewhat unrelated, as it were, some little disturbance between her and the world, that earned her partiality from everyone.

At all events, they stood in a row facing us at prayers: Mrs Allwood, Patty, Collings and Violet, in their blue morning dresses and aprons. In the afternoon, they would change into black dresses, white muslin aprons, and caps with streamers. In the afternoon, the air would feel a little heavier, voices quieter. The afternoon was different, you understand.

But at prayers I prayed, 'I will not suck my sponge again because I know it is wicked and that God is closely related to Grandpapa who will find out and there will be a pestilence and I will grow up with a red rash for all my life, and I won't be able to go on the stage or wear high heels.'

That day I think my grandparents told me about the Holy Shroud of Turin. It was important and seemed exciting, and I was glad I had begged forgiveness for the sin of sucking my sponge, which was probably as bad as 'knowing' someone.

But what I had learned about the Turin Shroud stayed in my head until I needed it, when I summoned it forth, rediscovered it and used it.

After lunch, we always lay on our beds in the Chichester night nursery. On the curtains, the scarlet poppy heads lifted away from their pale background, as unsettling as a wound, so immediate and fatal. I counted the poppy heads, and knew they would always be there, just as we would always be us, unfailing and constant, every one of us, looking the same, being the same, perhaps a bit growner-up.

I lay down in my nippy little Chilprufe knickers and

Liberty bodice, that made me look like an anxious grub, and I counted the poppy heads again.

When I was young, I bled poppy-scarlet with my beginnings. At Christmas, at Christmas. In the hospital I am made dirty and I must not tell, but live with their dirt for my life.

Every time I counted the poppy heads they came out different, and I thought, let it be time to get up or I'll be a volcano and some baby rats as well. And I thought of my grandfather, Benedict, and how lucky he was to share my name, and how *Alice in Wonderland* was his favourite book and he could recite the whole of it. It still wasn't time to get up and I thought of the best moment ever, when my grandmother read me *The Cuckoo Clock* before bed, and then I made myself into a volcano shape.

When we got home from Chichester, we were jump at the beginning of autumn, and the routine so joyously abandoned while we were away was disinterred once again. As we tumbled in at the front door, yellow-haired Lily, the nursery maid, was reading a movie magazine in the kitchen – I could see her through the door – and Nanny was coming downstairs with a wedge of counterfeit charm plastered on her face. The only one of us she wanted to see was my youngest brother, and she got quite bobbish when he lurched in, looking round for treats, in an obviously brackish romper suit. It was evidently somewhat restoring to both Nanny and Lily that we all needed 'a good clean-up' after the journey, for to be clean was to be purged and deodorised and only thus might we be recognised as 'little ladies and gentlemen'.

Phrases like: 'Who'll be a nice clean girl for Mummy?' or, 'Don't you *dare* go near that nasty dirty boy!' could usually be attributed to most nannies of that era, and were often as meaningless as a street cry. From the same source came remarks like, 'Under a gooseberry bush, where do you think?' and, 'Curiosity killed the cat', which were sprinkled with such warnings as 'Never speak to strangers', a saying that was never clarified satisfactorily. The Sunday papers, breathlessly read by Nanny and Lily in the kitchen while Mrs Paxford was having a lay-down without her apron, interpreted everything to them. It was perfectly clear what happened to children who said, 'Yes, please,' to strange gentlemen, although obscure to me as I hung in the kitchen doorway, not really wanting to know.

'It is thought,' read Nanny in an involved, vibrant voice that gave me a bilious feeling, 'it is thought that fourteen-year-old auburn-haired Daphne Barton said, "Yes, please," before she was—.' Nanny put her hand over her mouth so that she didn't have to hear herself say 'interfered with'. Then she said it. I conjectured. Wrongly. And yellow-haired Lily took a long plugged-up breath and said, 'Only fourteen, too – to be interfered with like that – and in daylight too.' She opened a kirby grip with her teeth and ground it into her scalp, and you could see she wasn't planning to say, 'Yes, please,' to any strangers herself. Once I heard her say primly: 'Not until I'm married.'

I remembered her saying that, as I ran upstairs, and I heard Nanny saying, 'Better not go on about it. That child's been hanging around for I don't know how long. Give her nightmares.'

Things became a deal more sensible the day Miss Alexander arrived. An austere and reliable governess, she came initially to make digestible the gap between nappies and cricket pads that can be so painful.

And, quite perceptibly, the household changed, the balance dipping and swaying, relationships curdling, the nursery becoming the schoolroom yet leaving its footsteps behind. Nanny contentious with the kitchen over a failure to procure her black pudding for tea, a coldness throughout the house and may I have a word with you, Madam? It's about . . .

Gradually things became more serene and Miss Alexander, contained and well-mannered, devised each day's occupation and its manageable pace without duress or dislocation.

She had her dinner on a tray, with her own folkweave table napkin, made by herself and grasped by a silver napkin ring. Her curtains, drawn across the sunset, were also made by her of folkweave material in various shades of green, of which she was very fond. Upon the walls were artistically arranged watercolours of India and the Highlands of Scotland, all beautifully executed by Miss Alexander herself. A small display of Benares brass shone upon a corner table. By her bed, with its cover of folkweave, and a green nightdress cover embroidered by her in satin stitch, was a Bible and a handsome shabby Shakespeare with smouldering photographs of Johnston Forbes Robertson, Irving, Ellen Terry and the like. By invitation I was allowed to go into Miss Alexander's room and look at it, sitting on the floor by the electric fire, and sometimes she talked about India where she had lived once. The indistinct snapshots of herself and her father on horseback might have been taken in Richmond Park, but for the trenchant glamour of the mountains behind them. I thought of my mother, who had danced with a young Maharajah at a ball in

India, and how I had wished it was me. The bright sari colours brushed my mind, and I felt the slow bruising of patchouli. In my mind India and I burned and fused together and became Siva. But we never went to India because they said it was too hot.

When I was too dicky to go to the PNEU school, it was not unpleasant to draw and write and paint and do lessons in the schoolroom. Miss Alexander and I sat each side of the table, through the window, summer scotching autumn still, digestive biscuits still kept in the Union Jack tin for elevenses, and Nanny with us yet a bit. And in her room, Nanny hummed and thought snugly about the knitting pattern sent by Greta, her friend, and expected by the tea-time post, and even wondered whether she wouldn't pop her hat on and go to the wool shop, just to have a look. Just a look. She couldn't buy until the pattern arrived, of course, but there wouldn't be any harm in just having a look. And while she was about it she might pop into the Bonbon Bar and get a quarter of Mintoes. She popped her hat on and popped her head into the schoolroom where I was executing a meticulous painting of Jack Point from *The Yeoman of the Guard* for my father's birthday.

'Just going down to see Mrs Tomlin at the wool shop,' she said, adding handsomely, 'Anything I can do for you, Miss Alexander?'

She was fulsome with Miss Alexander now, for the switch of balance had left behind no wounded self-esteem, nor had it jeopardised security, and Nanny's niche was unassailable for some time. She was even heard to say Miss Alexander was quite ladylike. The household had been whisked together by the kindliness and determination of our new governess and by the insistence on protocol that we learned was a hallmark of hers. There was, however, tension when Miss Alexander pointed out that my jodhpurs should be more close-fitting over the calf, and it appeared that Nanny knew sauce when she heard it, and tightened her lips. I thought, wallop, here we go. But of course Miss Alexander was right.

By half term I was well enough to go to the PNEU school, familiar, pleasant and humdrum, with allowances made for my occasional indispositions. Moreover it was near by, and this time I was allowed to go and come back on my own. I had asked and it was granted as long as I eschewed all, speaking to no one, however innocent in appearance.

And the flung-up sky of autumn met me as I left the school, and orange leaves lay singly on the ground like shavings. I picked up conkers and put them in my pocket and they cracked together as I walked. All Glorious Within, I thought, just like the hymn. Within my pocket is the Glorious Company of Conkers. I picked one out and stroked its satin rump against my cheek and thought, I will make doll's-house furniture with them, or I will keep them in my room and esteem them.

Leaves rushed like rags, away and down, and Christmas burned in my mind, the London winter, sooty and promising, and our hoopsticks rattling against the railings. Christmas at Eccleston Square with our London grandparents, who owned two most sumptuous lavatories robed in wall-to-wall mahogany, and blessed with a neat trapdoor to deposit all below, adroitly and with style – did not these sustain my admiration throughout the visit? And for those in need of intellectual stimulus, here was yet further luxury – a pile of *Geographical Magazine*s filled with pictures of bare black people. And I thought how intensely lucky were my grandparents.

Christmas Day in London, though pleasant, was predictably impaired by displays of pique caused by aunt-given scarves in a somewhat emotional mixture of colours such as brick-red and lavender, and though harsh coral necklaces were popular aunt-offerings, what one wanted was bullion. I hoped someone would give me a dagger, so that I could kill people a bit, but on the whole girls didn't get given daggers, so I always had to wait until we went back home to buy a rubber one with my Christmas money. Once or twice I bought a little toy pistol with caps, but that wasn't for killing, it was for the lovely smell of gunpowder from the caps.

Carlsbad Plums, indoor fireworks and the reedy vibrations of the gramophone closed the rents that often rupture Christmas afternoon, while my mother and her family, bookish and amusing, sat about bickering and laughing, filaments of smoke from their Turkish cigarettes curling round mantelpieces, and filching reflections of other Christmases. Norman, a brother, young in death, the Great War wrenching his mettle away, a packet of Turkish gaspers in his tunic pocket, perhaps. And a snapshot of a girl.

Christmas Day is well, is pleasant, I thought, as I walked along the road, but, oh, Boxing Day come to me, and Peter Pan. Be sure of me every year whether I grow up or whether I don't. But I must be sure of you, and you must always be Jean Forbes Robertson. Or I will fall and die in a London gutter and everyone will say, 'It needn't have happened. We should have made certain that she always saw Jean Forbes Robertson in

Peter Pan year after year after year and she could have led a full and happy life.'

If I am to live at all, I thought, caressing the conkers in my pocket, it is necessary that every Boxing Day matinée I see those nursery windows bursting open with that great gale of air for Peter to fly in like a dark animal that is certain of where it's going, but is unsure who its friends are. It gives me a funny split feeling. Which I like.

And I murmured, 'Oh, Peter, Peter, take me with you – I can fly, you know I can, don't have Wendy in that soppy little bonnet, I'll take care of you.'

But I felt that girls weren't right for Peters. Mothers perhaps – concerned, uncomprehending, and often very pleased and saying so. And of course, there. Drying their socks. But not getting in the way, like girls do.

Abruptly, from behind me, a man's voice said, 'You're a nice little girl,' and I jumped and turned round feeling my stomach curl, and a prickle of nerves under my skin. I looked at him and said nothing, since he might only have wanted to know the time. My throat felt strange and thick and I couldn't speak in any case.

I looked back at the empty road and began to walk faster.

'Going far?' he said. He was pacing me, and I didn't like it.

I shook my head.

He said: 'How about a cup of tea? I live near here.'

'I'm only allowed milk,' I said, adding, 'Thank you,' and I felt cold and frightened and deserted. He suggested I should come in for a sit-down, and said we were nearly there. And again he said what a nice little girl I was.

I said: 'No, I can't – I'm – I don't think my parents

would—' and the words ran away down my throat. When I looked at him there was something about him that made me want to give one big yell and run. 'I'll walk you home,' he said quickly, and I said, 'No. No, don't,' and I began to run. The road was empty. He caught me up and I shouted, 'Go away! I don't want to – what do you want? What is it?'

I stopped and stood, shivering a bit, and said loudly: 'If you don't go away, I'll call a policeman.' My voice sounded big and brave, and his face changed. He hesitated and I said, 'Go away at once.'

He said, 'Right, I will. Thanks for fucking nothing.' And he turned and walked away. And I remember the look of him walking away, the afternoon small and dark.

And I remember how I ran in at the side gate and through the kitchen where Lily was reading a movie magazine. And on the dresser was a drawing I'd done of Ginger Rogers for Lily to put up in her bedroom. And I thought, You didn't, did you, yellow-haired Lily? Luckily I don't hate you, I'll simply give it to someone else. And I remember the door of the larder was open, and I looked in as I hurtled past and thought, pity only scones, no Shrewsbury biscuits, never mind, because I felt better, and braver and taller.

So I went up into the schoolroom with quite a bit of bounce for my gallantry, and Miss Alexander was writing letters. Taking her specs off and pinching the bridge of her nose, she said: 'You're a bit late, pet.' And I felt a lessening of my strutting, a cooling, as though perhaps there had never been much to swagger about anyway. So I put off telling her, and said I was late because of the conkers, which I took out of my pocket, and put on to the table. I felt a thump of fear inside me again and wondered if I had done something wrong. Miss Alexander said: 'You look a bit peelie-waulie, are you all right, dear?' So I told her. And all those feelings I'd had before leaped up into me again, and I felt sick and silly. Her face was disabled by alarm suddenly, and she told me to go and lie on my bed, and that she would get my mother.

Perhaps I'm ill, I thought as I got into bed. Or maybe naughty. Who will tell me?

I was neither. But I was certainly a matter for concern, and had already heard yellow-haired Lily say, 'The poor chowd', in a voice choked with anticipation, and Mrs Paxford asking Miss Alexander if I might manage some raspberry jelly. Nanny would have been thrilled if she hadn't been at an autumn jumble sale.

My mother came in, clearly racked with worry, but insufferably beautiful nonetheless. I loved her and felt much better at once, comforted by the panache with which she stubbed out a cigarette in the cowrie shell saucer that I'd won at the fair. She said: 'Now, darling,' and moving to the mantelpiece, rearranged my coloured Shirley Temple postcards. I didn't mind about the saucer. You could wash it.

She came and sat beside my bed and stroked my forehead and asked me whether I was all right, and I said I was. I didn't know her very well, and she seemed distressed and didn't look at me very much. So I waited, and she said, 'Nothing? I mean—?' and I said, 'No. Really, really nothing, Mummy.'

I stroked her hand and thought, oh Mummy, if it is so awful for you, then just don't say anything. I expect it's what I've found out about anyway, so you don't need to worry. She said she'd noticed I'd grown up a bit, and I said, yes I had. Then she said, 'Darling,' and I said, 'Yes,' and she said, 'You know it really is quite important not to talk to anyone you don't know. Now tell me exactly what happened.' So I did, and she looked out of the window and I think she felt much better. She had some of my raspberry jelly and said it was just right for the way she was feeling.

Before she went out of the room, I said: 'Would you say I'm grown up now? Or would you not say so?'

And she said: 'Well, I would not really say so – not absolutely. On the other hand, I wouldn't say you were not grown up either. Shall we say grown up to an extent. Why?'

And I said: 'Well, am I grown up enough to use the other lav after breakfast instead of going to the one the younger ones use? It would make me feel grander, and I need that kind of grandness, oh please, you and Daddy have your own, oh why not?'

'Oh, darling . . .,' she said with a great sigh. 'Really, really, really, I don't think that is at all important, you know how Nanny likes everything to stay the same, it makes her feel more secure, do be sensible. Settle down darling, and be a good dog. You've had a bit of a shock, but you mustn't expect the whole world to change.'

As she shut the door, I shouted, 'Then why is everyone making a big fuss of me – I mean jelly and terrific talking and everything?' She looked back round the door and said: 'Darling. We love you, and we've been worried about you, that's all, nothing to get uppity about, and nothing that's earned you any concessions.' And she blew a kiss.

Next morning at breakfast I said I had a weasel in my plate of Force, but nobody took any notice at all.

'I don't think I'm going to eat my Force today,

because of the weasel that's lying asleep in it. I don't want to wake it up, because I'm always kind to weasels. As long as they're kind to me,' I said fatuously, 'and they always are because there's something special about me. I have strange powers. That's why weasels lie curled up in my Force.' John said, 'I'd rather have a rhinoceros in mine. They're quite sweet, and they don't show off like weasels.'

David spat a rusk on to the table and Nanny stroked his cheek and said: 'Isn't he lovely?' and John said, 'How disgusting,' and I said, 'I shouldn't think he'll ever get jelly for being marvellous, like me. I think I shall cook some Plasticine after breakfast.'

'I'll give you cook Plasticine,' said Nanny, doing an enthusiastic fart as she went into the night nursery, and John said, 'Not very ladylike.'

'That'll do,' said Nanny, coming back, adding, 'And no, you may not cook Plasticine. The idea.'

'My mother', I said, 'has told me. That I can use the other lav, now that I am older. AND. She says it is bad for me to use the children's lav, because of being delicate. And. She says I must have Bromo paper and not Bronco, which is—.'

'Don't be silly, she never said anything of the sort,' said Nanny. 'You'll do exactly as you're told. Having a governess doesn't mean you can behave la-di-da. What makes you think you're the Duchess of Dresden, I'd like to know? Your baby brother doesn't go on like that, now does he? Very well then, say grace and you may get down.'

So we said Thank God for my good breakfast, please may I get down, and I asked Nanny if I could wear my new shoes for a bit to make up for not being allowed to cook Plasticine, and oh, for goodness' sake, yes, what next I'd like to know. So of course I went to the usual old lav without a murmur.

Afterwards John said, 'Why did you have jelly yesterday? What happened?'

'I'm not allowed to talk about it,' I said. 'It's something special that only happens to certain people, and I'm one of them.'

I put my new shoes on and my feet were ennobled by them, and I was made wonderful by them and noticeable. But I was not noticed, even when I did different kinds of walks.

The morning loosened, unlacing slowly, as a woman prises her stays from her at night, limbering herself for pleasure. Stretching and murmuring, her early thoughts are blunted, and rings dropped on a dressing table, like raindrops. The need is joyfully and fiercely subjugated.

I wore my new shoes, and wondered how long the day would last. The morning opened for us, and we sprang into it with a trembling certainty, and against the big top's darkness, I felt the catch of hands save me, and the turn of a wheel mark me.

I ran up and down stairs, my new shoes as bonny as cherry skins, as eye-catching as I might be soon, soon, soon, and in the hall my fervent, emotional jumping about made me fall down quite often. I felt my life might change because of my new shoes, as I used to hope for it when I was older and wearing a new frock.

But nothing. Darting about in my cherry shoes, all over the garden, in an empty world is what I was doing. And right away down on the bit that was meant to be a tennis court I could see John turning somersaults in the summer buzz, a muff of gnats throbbing round him, his shorts slumping off his hips.

'See my new shoes!' I hollered, and he didn't answer,

played being an aeroplane, didn't look at me, or notice or anything.

My mother, examining roses for greenfly, a cigarette in her mouth, said: 'Darling, do you think you should wear your new shoes all the time?' And I gave a long dog-howl and threw a great punch into a rose bush, and, bloodied, went indoors.

As I went upstairs I thought, Hallowed be my shoes. But I said to Nanny: 'I don't really care for these shoes after all, and I told Mummy I wouldn't wear them today, and she said of course.' I don't know why I said this, the words scrapped about inside my head, and I knew they weren't true. And I took off the shoes and went into the linen cupboard and leaned my head against a shelf, and I cried small crying. When I came out I felt as if I would probably manage.

Nanny was being a bit fancy that day because her sister was coming over for the afternoon, and we must all behave properly. And because of this sister, we had to have our afternoon walk in the morning. Whatever the time of day, the drive seethed with imprisoned darkness, the laurels stirring and clattering in steep banks each side.

I stuck to the pram, to John, to the dogs of war, even to Nanny, until we got out of the gate. First into Meavy Lane, lagging behind the pram to pick wild strawberries, so small and sudden and sweet in the dark bank. And so forbidden to eat, like music in one's mouth. I handed some to John, who squashed one against his shirt, a small brilliant wound. I said: 'Clean it with spit, or she'll be cross, with her old sister coming.' He tried, but it was still there, so he kept his hand over it for a bit.

We got up to the moor, and it swam round us, dark

and raw even on that summer's day, occasionally a sullen blanket of fog settling round the village like a shawl, and round the gaunt house we had to live in then, in Devon, because my father was stationed there.

'What's that on your shirt, John?' said Nanny, with a sudden notch in her voice.

'Blood,' said John, and Nanny said, 'Don't be silly,' but looked worried.

'It is,' said John. 'I got stabbed by someone.'

'More like a bullet wound, I'd say.' I examined it, and Nanny smacked my hand down. You and your sister, I thought, I hope you fall down and everyone sees your knickers.

And John and I let her and the pram and the dogs go on ahead, and we stayed.

I stood still, and felt as though something murmured inside me, as though something tried to comfort me. I wished my parents were there and I looked up at the sky. There was a sudden thickness in the air, and drops of water spat down on us. Barbs of sunlight cut through the darkness here and there like promises, but stopped as suddenly as a last breath.

'I thought it was going to be a storm!' I shouted, but I couldn't see John. 'I got all those funny feelings, all jumpy and excited and frightened. I love it, I really love it. But then it stopped.'

He was looking at something on the ground by a little scrubby bush, and he said: 'Come on, there's something here you ought to see. Buck up.'

'What is it?' I said. It was surging about and there was a terrible smell as well. John didn't answer.

I said, 'Is it alive?'

He said, 'No. It's dead. Stinky as well, because of maggits. It's only a dead bird.'

46

'I think I'm going to be sick,' I said.

'Right,' said John. 'Leave it and come on. It's only a dead old bird,' and we walked on. But I felt sad as well as sick, and I thought, oh Mummy I'm afraid. I didn't like it, but I had to look, and it's made the day different. I said: 'Does that happen to people as well?'

And my brother wanted to make me feel better, so he said: 'It happens to railway engines, I can tell you,' so I hit him and he felled me to the ground, and Nanny said, 'That'll do,' without turning round.

Running. Running away. Oh Mummy, they catch me, caught me, netted me, tripped and trapped the wound in me forever.

We trailed home. The flock of geese that wheeled and honked round the lawn were, of course, an impulse buy of my mother's, and as unproductive and invincible as storm-troopers, charging the callow backs of our knees, as we fled past the stables and in at the front door yelling: 'Get out, rats, get out!'

We had to get shined up after lunch, with Nanny's sister coming, but also with awful Hope Millington coming to tea.

She was not awful enough to remark upon, merely having a formidable nullity, the bleached face and lashless eyes suggesting, not unattractively, Rogier van der Weyden's 'Portrait of a Young Lady'. Thus she appeared clement, and surely was unspotted. And you felt you could see through her limpid eyes to the back of her head without the faintest chance of encountering any brains.

She needs a treat, I thought. She is not so bad; she shall meet my ill bat in the outhouse, she will enjoy that. And we walked down to the bat's outhouse, I in my brother's grey shorts and snake belt and Hope in a clean cotton frock. Her mouth was as neat as a pod, the small double chin moderate, and somehow agreeable.

'Want to see my ill bat?' I said. She moved her hands along the top of the gate, and did not answer for a moment. Then she said, 'When will it be tea?' 'Soon,' I said. 'When we've seen my bat. He gets lonely. He likes visitors. Come on.'

'Are bats kind?' she said.

I said: 'Well. I don't really – yes, they're really sweet. Come on. Then you'll see.'

She climbed carefully over the gate, in her blue frock with a white collar, and we walked to the doorway of the outhouse and looked in. Like a little undertaker, my bat hung from the rafters. 'There,' I said. 'Isn't he lovely? Of course he's not feeling very well at the moment. You ought to see him when he's all right, he's very kind of frisky then.'

There was quite a long pause, then she said: 'He doesn't look kind, like you said. Are they fierce? Are you sure they don't bite?'

I had to say yes, though I'd been bitten on my left thumb, which swelled up and the mark is still there. I hadn't let on to Nanny though – I didn't want to get my bat into trouble.

Hope said: 'Its head. It looks like a little dog's head. Does anyone know you've got it here? How do you feed it?'

'Bits from lunch. He doesn't eat much, and he's not well anyway. Do you like him?'

'Not much,' said Hope. 'I mean what does he do?'

'When he's well again, I'll teach him tricks – he likes that,' I said. I wished she could go home and said: 'Let's go in, otherwise it's just never going to be time for you to go home.' It wasn't really what I meant to say, and I hoped she had not heard. But when I looked at her, it was as though her small economical face had undergone some kind of reshuffle, and I wondered if perhaps she was not very much liked by anyone, and knew it. Since I was not particularly popular myself, I understood and was worried, looking at her often and anxiously, and praying that she had misheard me.

As we passed the stables, I tried to make up for my boorishness by asking her if she would like to see my father's polo ponies. She said no, thank you, she wouldn't, and we went indoors. As we got to the stairs, I said: 'Have you enjoyed yourself?' She considered for a moment and said: 'Well, not really. You see I don't really care much for animals, and that bat was a bit frightening. Are you sure you're allowed to keep it there?'

I found it rather difficult to answer that, so I said: 'We're having fairy cakes for tea because of you and Ivy.'

'Who's Ivy?' she said, and when I told her it was Nanny's sister, she started laughing. I'd never seen her laugh before – she put her hands over her mouth and laughed all the way upstairs. It was the name, she said – Ivy – and she went on laughing. I did not think it funny, but her features were so ordered that each seemed to swap one with the other when she laughed, charming and amusing me. Thus, I had merely to whisper, 'Ivy', to Hope for her to lean against me, buckling us both to the floor, and our behaviour being unaccountable, I apologised grandiosely to Nanny. I was not allowed a fairy cake, but Hope, her eyes watering and with an apologetic glance at me, took two, ducking her head over her plate.

Now I found her pleasant, for what can bind the spirits as potently as the ligature of laughter? But as time passed, it seemed caprice, and when we met again, we did not charm each other, and her face, waxen and frugal, did not rouse itself if I murmured 'Ivy'. She turned from me, asking only what was for tea, not wishing to see my bat, nor anything.

Several times she came, for we were thought to be friends, and her mother, an old friend of my mother's, came to collect her, with an appearance of great embarrassment that naturally caused us to be embarrassed. It was as though she felt responsible for something she could not own to. She sat in the drawing room, drinking sherry, and her oblong brown skirt made me think of a piece of luggage. Mrs Millington had a thrilling bell-like voice, and to be honest she sounded like a pack of hounds, particularly from a few miles away. Each time Hope came, Mrs Millington collected her, and each time she asked me if we had had nice games, and I looked at my mother and said we had.

Eventually, Hope and I ceased to see each other except at children's parties, at which Mrs Millington wore wool-embroidered skirts and peasant blouses with drawstring necks. From her drooping neck depended savage flame-coloured necklaces and large rolled gold lockets. She showed intensity over the bran tubs and treasure hunts and was not often asked to help. But remained smiling.

A visit to London to stay with our distaff grandparents was attended by a considerable *bouleversement*. First, Nanny went on a short holiday and we were nonplussed to find ourselves with a French nanny with B.O. and little English, although quite nice. My mother climbed to the top of the house to drum the lingo into our heads, and we were quite glad to get our original Nanny back.

Miss Alexander left for a holiday with relations in Scotland, in tweeds, ghillie shoes, a hat with a feather in it, and with egg sandwiches in greaseproof paper. She would be temporarily replaced by one Miss Layton, to which end she first stripped her own room to the bone, since Miss Layton would sleep there and might turn out to be a thief. 'I shouldn't imagine she'll need my nightdress case,' she said, picking it up, and looking challengingly round the room. 'I think I'll put the Benares away,' she added. 'I've left her a few drawers, and there are some coat hangers in the wardrobe. Well, I hope you manage.'

We did manage. But we missed her greatly, and she knew we would.

Miss Layton took us by surprise, so to speak. She was extremely tall, and had something of the appearance of a giraffe, even to the markings – the smudges of brown having moved together in precisely that manner, though I fancy they were freckles in her case. She had the look of one who had perhaps faded in the wash – it was difficult to imagine that she or her clothes had ever had an original colour or pattern. Though hardly sustaining, yet she was jocund and anxious to do anything one wanted, jumping up to say, 'Yes, let's!' with a good many things falling off her lap. Her eyes were blue, but since they had a slightly opaline quality, it was difficult to attribute sight to them.

She never talked about her family or private life, simply jamming on a cloche hat before she left for her half-day, and saying: 'Well, cheerio, children!' to which, being snobs, we said: 'Goodbye.'

She always came back at about seven o'clock, looking

much as she had when she left, and with a cold supper waiting in her room. One day she didn't come back. Not at all. And when they found her, she'd been murdered. But my mother didn't tell us until we were grown up. She was rather nice, and we were sorry when she didn't come back. Still.

After such a how d'ye do, we were rushed to London as soon as possible. And I sat in my grandfather's study in Eccleston Square, leaning against his knee and stroking his elephant table, for steeply carved and in insufferable taste, it was all I really lusted after, and I could not touch it without experiencing a dark, sinful clamour inside me. This was wicked, I knew, and prayed that it could not be detected by those looking at me. The glory of the elephant table lay in its four perfect elephant heads, so truthful that surely one touch from me would transform the obdurate wood into the touching demeanour and suppliant trunk of a real elephant. Like my mother's elephant in India. Lovingly I counted the four heads, one at each corner, and leaned my head against my chosen elephant, as we moved ponderously through the steaming jungle.

My grandfather's gramophone records of Galli Curci ground on, and the great umbilical creepers of the liana caught at my hair as I lay low against my elephant's head, the shadow of the peepul tree darkening us both. Little twigs cracked beneath his measured steps, and round us was the fitful scoffing of the brain-fever bird.

Faint with desire, I breathed, 'Oh, Grandpapa, let me have one head to take home with me. They're so sweet. Please, just one.'

Just one, he said, would cause the disintegration of the entire table.

'It's their trunks I love, oh please, I could put food in

52

their mouths. Perhaps if I'm good I could have the whole table? Could I?'

'Where would I put my books?' he said. 'And the gramophone? And besides, I'm fond of it.'

We were silent. I pointed at the 'Pied Piper' made of butterflies' wings, and asked if I might have that, perhaps.

'Perhaps, but not yet though. I'm fond of that as well. Get out the chess pieces,' he said, 'and let's see if we can teach you to play. If not, well, it'll do no harm to do a bit of talking instead.'

We did a bit of talking instead. 'Tell about being a Member of Parliament,' I said.

'It's interesting. Got to keep your wits about you,' he said.

'Tell about how you deal with the Commons when they're fractious,' I said.

'Again?'

I said: 'Yes. I love it.'

He got up and said: 'Then I will tell you how the Commons can be discomposed by a few words.'

I said: 'Go on.'

'Let us assume', he said, 'that the House is in uproar over some hen-brained *idée fixe*. Would you advise me to take instant action, my dear child?'

'I would not, Grandpapa.'

'You are right. Circumspection must be exercised. And then, rising to my feet and waiting for the hubbub to subside, I say, simply: "I question that statement." It is unnecessary to say anything further. There is a moment's silence during which I resume my seat, and then, my dear child – pandemonium. For those words invariably reveal some error – sometimes a mere *lapsus linguae*, but occasionally something more serious. It is a

53

strategy, of course, but I have never known it fail, and I have never found it necessary to say anything further. And if concealment is suspected, then it is your right to ask the questions that will flush out the truth. And don't be afraid of getting your hands dirty either. Why do you bite your nails, my dear?' Abashed, I said nothing.

And Grandpapa said: 'I think we can do much better than that. Go down to the dining room – there's a tin of guava jelly there from my sea captains. Bring it here, and a teaspoon.'

And when I left the study, I felt the sounds and scents of Lucia, his first wife and dead, whose name I carried too, perhaps half Italian and unaccustomed to the blur of London. She taught my mother how to play the tambourine in the proper way, and my mother taught me in a dark nursery, the wet railings of the square outside shining like liquorice.

Did she, Lucia, did she lightly steal into the study where later I caressed the elephant?

'Austin?' did she say, he younger, she cold from the great house and the stairwell, and touching his hair.

He might say: 'What will you wear tonight?' And she would lift her arms, and look in the glass and laugh, and say: 'I will wear white, certainly, and the sapphire necklace you gave me.'

And perhaps he says: 'Lucia, I don't want anything to happen to you. Ever.'

She says: 'Don't be silly. Something happens to all of us,' but she says it like a child who doesn't believe it, and shivers.

'I am cold,' she says. 'How can you sit in this room, it is so sparse. Do you really like it?'

And he says: 'I love it,' and gives a great laugh.

But Lucia died quite young, and we did not meet,

nor did I know how she had died, and there was no asking in the shadowed pauses of tea-time conversation.

Sometimes the sisters spoke of her: 'Mother might have—' or 'Mother didn't—' they would say, leaving a farthing of silence to check questioning. Which was not allowed, of course – but minds hopped through hoops of chance. For nobody ever spoke about Lucia. Perhaps it was a hunting accident that took her, for in a photograph, a stocky groom in shirtsleeves and billy-cock hat holds a stubby little pony by a rein. But nothing is betrayed, and our grandfather is wounded, forever it seems, although he married again to kiss it better and for comfort.

And the sisters sit in the drawing room for tea, and say nothing, and we sit in the schoolroom with the musical box and the painting of Norman and say nothing.

I see the draggled riding-habit as Lucia is carried back to the house. Greenholme it would be. The horse stumbles and the light goes. Someone is dispatched for the doctor. 'Run, boy!'

But he is already into the dark, the boy, and breathing rough, dismay and fearfulness strengthening his blub-bered Our Fathers, piped in the little school for just this day's dark finishing.

But now there is no simple certainty for us to reach, and, since we did not ask, we have only the guess. So Lucia, perhaps brushed still with the warm slow drench of the olive's oil, began to take puzzled pleasure in musical evenings, and young men who said, 'Just the ticket.'

In the large coloured photograph, she looks young, composed, informed. Neither pretty nor beautiful, but distinctive, guarding her intelligence as though she feels hazarded by it. Something caught at her sleeve once perhaps, and never let her go without a tag of fitfulness and conflict, a dissonance that may have been shuttered a little.

Round her left wrist a piece that I believe to be uncharacteristic of the time, a heavy gold chain bracelet, hanging from it a large gold key, and what might be a gold padlock. In her right hand, slight and strong, is caught the sapphire necklace.

Lucia brought forth one son and three daughters. Norman died unseasoned in the Great War – half-inched from life by the yammer of enemy fire.

Of the daughters, Dorothea stayed at home, wearing cardigans and shell necklaces in what my grandfather called 'obstinate bad taste'. She was kind, intelligent, and a little tedious, and we were very fond of her. When she grew older she plumped for archetypal ladies' clothes from Woollands, and at her club translated the menu for you.

Gifted, emancipated and argumentative, Barbara learned sculpture in Rome, firmly licking me into shape years later in her Chelsea studio. While my mother, an enterprising and formidable young woman of great beauty, likewise studied in Rome, painted under Sickert, and upon a challenge from her uncle, a judge, became a best-selling authoress in her early twenties.

This uncle, Sir Francis Taylor, asked me to lunch at the Inner Temple in my late teens.

Assuming that a distinguished judge's great-niece must not give the impression of a life of pleasure, I presented myself to Uncle Frank in a less than succulent outfit in beige tweed, little make-up, and of course no scent, which would have been marked as fast. A somewhat unpromising felt hat obscured my face, and Uncle

Frank, startled, fell back apace. Since he knew I was going on the stage after the war, he was expecting something like the lead in *Gay Rosalinda*, not a gamekeeper, and conversation was as parched and sparing as a rusk.

After I had drunk quite a deal of wine, one or two things happened rather quickly, probably because I was, at that age, unaccustomed to it. The first thing that happened was that a strikingly dramatic and perpendicular shard of venison placed before me was too intractable to get my fork into, and in the attempt, my hat caught on a vase each time I bent forward, taking several minutes to disentangle, success only being achieved by Uncle Frank. Since a few spring flowers had transferred themselves from the vase to my hat, it is hardly necessary to add that I spilled my plums and custard on the tablecloth in front of me, and in an effort to set matters to rights knocked over my wineglass.

Although Uncle Frank and I were now laughing quite openly, he did not draw attention to my blotto behaviour, but got me some black coffee, lent me half a crown for the taxi, and said how much he had enjoyed everything. And suggested I have a nap when I got home.

Naturally, I hoped every man who took me out to lunch would be as attractive as Uncle Frank, and naturally I did not mention having been sozzled when I wrote him a Collins. But neither did he mention it when he wrote telling my mother how charming and intelligent I was, suggesting, however, that a decent dress allowance might be appropriate at my age. Young women, he said, should not be condemned to wear such despondent clothes.

'I think he was expecting you to turn up looking like

the Merry Widow,' said my mother. 'Next time, wear what you would for a young man.'

But there wasn't a next time, because Uncle Frank was already getting on then. But still. Still, one of the nicest.

When I was about eight, and stood in the drawing room at Eccleston Square, I felt the eager vandalising sea of Malta strain and buffet against me like love. But it was the slant of memory I think, and the craving to go back to the rocky heat and the quick lizards. The London weather shoves thick against the windows, and inside is a soirée, and my mother says I can wear my moderate finery, and stay up for an hour or two. Lucia's successor, Gaggle, married my grandfather. She is clenched in stays and winking with diamonds, and I will marry Catchlove the butler. Gaggle kicks the train backwards with a little punishing shoe, and I am in my party velvet and Vandyke collar.

Catchlove brings in the Rossmoyne Jelly that is made with burgundy and cream and hundreds and thousands, and I look at him and think, 'I will be constant, Catchlove.' And I am introduced to literary lions who ruffle my hair, and laugh and call me 'young lady'. But oh, Catchlove, marry me. Please. We will live in a bungalow with some dogs and gooseberry fool. Darling Catchlove, I will marry you in a pink frock, and you need not wear your butler's gloves, and if you like you can wear grey shorts for the wedding. Whatever you feel most comfortable in.

But the abandonment of weather dodged about outside like an interloper, and I thought oh, soon soon Malta, and soon Luigi and soon my lizard, and let me, bring me into the cool water, diving through a dark crystal. In three weeks, jump we will be there, hating our topees, loving the little orange trees with the sour oranges. And my lizard Joseph, who may still be alive. And the vines.

'I am going to bed. Are we going soon to Malta?' I said to my mother outside the drawing room.

'Very soon,' she said. 'Yes. Go to bed, my darling.'

'Sing "Goodbye Dolly Gray". Please,' I said. She sang it.

'And "We Don't Want to Lose You",' I said. She sang both of them, songs of her war, intrepid and sentimental, the sort of Tommy Atkins heroism that would swing us into the next war, but without the same songs. Her war was barely over. And I was born into the Jazz Age.

I didn't marry Catchlove, because he was run over and killed posting a letter for my grandfather. The household mourned and I wept for weeks, remembering the night of the soirée and the Rossmoyne Jelly and my moderate finery.

After that night was over, I thought of Malta and the day we would go on the P & O Liner, and of Joseph, my lizard. But that night, when I had said goodnight to my mother, I went downstairs to the empty schoolroom that was not really ours, and sat on the little old rocking horse and I heard the laughing and the music in the drawing room. I put the light on and listened to the aged musical box. Its missing tines gave a wounded sound to its plangency, and 'See the Conquering Hero Comes' seemed in shock. I stood and looked at the painting of young, dead Norman, feeling only a strangeness and a flying curiosity that I could dismiss by turning my head. There was still noise coming from the kitchen in the basement.

When the hall clock strikes ten, then I must go up to Nanny. I sit on the floor, pulling books from the revolving bookcase, and a tumble of them fall on the floor. Hazlitt, Ruskin, Emerson and Butler, all allowed me and all familiar. I choose Ruskin's *Sesame and Lilies*, and tussle with it for a little while until the clock strikes.

At the foot of the stairs is Catchlove.

'You look beautiful, Catchlove,' I say.

He replies: 'So do you, Miss.'

'Oh, thank you. Will there be any Rossmoyne Jelly left for tomorrow tea-time in the schoolroom?'

'I'm afraid not, Miss. There were fifty guests tonight, you see. All hungry too, I should say.'

In the night nursery, Nanny undoes my Liberty bodice. 'Enjoy it?' she says without interest. 'Fairly,' I say. 'They weren't real lions, though, worse luck, only literary ones. Long hair and poetry.'

'Shame,' says Nanny, disposed to be pleasant with half a bottle of stout and a specially ordered black pudding inside her. As I get into bed, I say: 'We are going shopping in the motor car with Gaggle tomorrow. I shall be wearing a long dress and ballet shoes.'

'That'll do,' she says, and snaps off the light. 'I hate you, Nanny Farnell,' I whisper.

Very thick and mauve was the face powder of our step-grandmother Gaggle as she stepped from the house to the car. She stepped quickly, but trembled a little, and held her head somewhat to one side. A front of silver curls affixed to her forehead caused a resemblance to the Minotaur, and a black crushed velvet toque suggested royalty. She smiled at Simmons, the chauffeur, who stood holding the rug. Once she was inside the car, she removed her gloves and adjusted the veil beneath her chin. We jumped in after her, plunging about under the rug like blind puppies, our futures secure and milky, our outlook bosky, pastoral and footloose.

Since there was a glass division between us and Simmons, the motor car did not move until Gaggle had picked up the speaking tube to say 'Harrods please, Simmons.' And even then you hardly noticed it start.

Her hand looked like creased tissue paper, and when I took it, it felt like another child's hand, but cool and still. She sat little taller than me, slightly exalted by the toque. I looked at her and loved her, for, though in her late sixties, she was no step away from being a child herself. We wrought no efforts from each other, and felt few differences. We knew where we were with one another, and that it was perfectly in order to expect violet cachous to suck in the car, provided this expectation did not approach carnal passion. Not that we discussed this, but it would have been difficult to imagine her shaken by any such emotion even when young.

Gaggle, Eccleston Square, and London were luxury, grandeur, riches far beyond pocket money. Gaggle's philosophy was formidably simple – everyone should look pretty, enjoy themselves, and have plenty to look forward to. And our visit to Eccleston Square meant several mornings spent at Harrods toy department with our step-grandmother, who happily allowed dolls' clothes and trains to be put on her account, and whose vocation was, in any case, shopping, and whose pleasure was the sight of a stream of delivery vans bowling up to the house. She carried no purchases, had never heard of a shopping bag, and seldom walked anywhere. Should she do so, crowds divided like the Red Sea, and the place became black with bobbies springing to protect one they assumed to be visiting royalty.

If she appeared complacent about these attentions, I suspect that it was partly that she had grown accustomed to them, and partly that she had hardly noticed what had taken place, thus thanking cab drivers, coppers and passers-by for their help, without much idea of what it had entailed. And a fragile naiveté protected her from any show of pique. Seldom out of humour, she was devoted to children, whom wisely she encountered only when she wished, and likewise we were charmed by her, though her absence frequently went unmarked. The relationship being thus without constraint on either side, proved satisfactory to both.

I encountered other people's butlers upon whose silver salvers Gaggle placed her calling cards, when I went with her to other drawing rooms for seedcake and tiny conversations that fell like spilled trinkets that were not retrieved. If, when we arrived, we were not welcome, the butler murmured that his mistress was 'not at home', thus clearing the moment of embarrassment, and we would leave for our next objective. If the wind was in the right quarter, and the words 'at home' were heard, we climbed the many stairs in the wake of the parlour maid, or perhaps the butler, to a dim close drawing room, which smelt, one might say, of rich old ladies. The furniture seemed not so much arranged, as dealt, like a pack of cards, round the room, discouraging speech, but for the occasional plummet of small separate words that recoiled too soon to beam much interest on to the cabal.

Swinging my legs even for the short span allowed for calls was irksome, and for me the most entertaining ploy was simply to remove the entire scene and slot it into the back of my memory. At this stage it always appeared like a scene in a model theatre. But when I got home, or sometimes many years ahead, I would take out and play back this scrutiny in my head, and at varying speeds, perhaps catching certain details that had eluded me earlier on. On the whole, I always kept this kind of thing locked. Unless I needed it.

Aunt Fanny, upon whom we sometimes called, disconcerted me, although it was not easy to say why. She was plump and seemed altogether unable to move from her armchair in the corner of the drawing room, indeed perhaps never did. Each time we saw her, she appeared to have recently sustained some minor disaster. Nothing shocking, you understand, merely something in the nature of her foot being caught in a bandstand and imprisoning her for twenty-four hours in a snowstorm. Or a sweep inadvertently emptying his brush over her, or perhaps the doctor having to come and remove a caraway seed from her ear.

She always appeared about to recount something of this kind, but of course she never quite did, her light-weight voice merely giving an occasional cry of despair which seemed to fatigue her, though not greatly. A dusty glass case stood in the room, in it, arranged upright, her late husband's uniform, the shouts and spume of battle plucked from its scarlet and gold, the sword a mute attestor to conjectured bravery. I believed in the painted sward surrounding it, and would have touched it, finding no shame in gallantry, and thinking its stillness worthy. But the glass forbade such prying.

Coming home in the car, I usually slept heavily against Gaggle after an afternoon of calling. I leaned against the black velvet bosom and the kid gloves, and took from the slight stuffiness of the car and the scent

of violet cachous my childhood's particular safe-
keeping, and the knowledge that nothing could do
me or my brothers harm. This certainty caught at
me, comfortably and reassuringly, long after it was
begged for.

Sleeping and waking, the day we would board the P &
O Liner for Malta swung in and out of my mind, and I
thought of the brilliant sea and the rocks. I thought of
the goats and my lizard, that might be alive still. I
thought of the small amount of hot school, and all the
great swimming that lay stretched ahead in the day that
was ours in a cool glory that was happy and permissive.

There was always the chance that I might be ill, I
thought, but if so, I hoped it would only be once, and it
would be the same doctor and the same pattern, and I
would not mind.

During the last few days before we left, I thought of
Malta as I did each time we went – with an almost
terrible intensity, until suddenly the waiting had finished, the voyage had begun and ended and we were
there in Sliema at the house with the pepper tree, that
was not really called that at all.

We went through the great big gate, past the pepper
tree and up the path. My lizard streaked out of his crack
in the wall of the house. His paw was obviously better,
and oh! true-hearted lizard, he smiled at me, I am certain
of it.

'O upright lizard!' I said, and touched one of his feet,
which flickered.

My brother said: 'Upright what?'

I fell down, and got up again at once, so that my
brother would think I'd done it on purpose and I said it

was 'lizard' and Shakespeare, and that it was more than some people were.

The sun swooped and burned through our skins and right inside, and oh Mummy, please let's go down to Tigne and swim, let's cut through the water and burn and freeze and stay there forever and not go back to England. Small-walled gardens, three of them for us children to play in, with young orange trees and green oranges to wither our tongues. But in the big garden for grown-ups, I sat with Mme Davy to do French lessons with little splashes of sun starting through the vines on to us.

My legs ached and swung, and my thick handmade sandals hung away from my feet. Mme Davy and I always did French at a table set upon the terrace, with the tangle and scramble of the big old vine roofing us a little.

Mme Davy wore a mauve blouse, and a mauve crochet hat, and had a slight moustache. Always she brought with her a black shopping bag, generally with nothing in it. She shopped on the way back, and spoke almost no English, so her life seemed committed to silently teaching small girls French and wordlessly shopping in English-speaking shops in Sliema. Sometimes we smiled at one another, occasionally she slapped a mosquito away with a little sound of exasperation, turning to smile at me, in case I should feel in any way included in the slap.

In front of us on the table lay, open, a French grammar, an exercise book and *Les Malheurs de Sophie*. An earthenware pitcher of barley water stood within our reach, covered with a circle of muslin, weighted down with blue beads.

I said: '*Voici le livre que vous avez demandé,*' and Mme

Davy said: '*Bien, mon enfant,*' yawning and smiling. She was a very nice woman and we liked her, though I was daunted by her sudden unfamiliar behaviour when almost choking to death on a grape pip. Since she choked extremely slowly and almost deliberately, I stood with my mouth open for seconds before I realised what was happening. Slowly she rose, and slowly wove this way and that, like a May bug, and with terrible sounds she hurtled towards the wall of the house, where she leaned for some moments, with regular rasping noises coming from her.

I knew that if I did not conquer my inertia, she would simply throb to death before my eyes on the terrace, and I would be hung.

Screaming, I ran through the French windows, and yelled: 'Mummy, if you don't come, Madame will be dead!'

My mother instantly rose from the sofa in a cloud of eau-de-Cologne and summoned her experiences from the First World War. With a burst of impressive but incorrect French, she approached and grasped Madame, and, without delay, dealt her an annihilating blow between the shoulder blades. She then sat Madame upright in a chair and sent me for a glass of water, not barley water, which might catch in the throat.

When it was over, and Madame had gone, I went through the stone doorway to one of our little gardens, with a spew of pampas in one corner and a little orange tree in the middle. On the way, Luigi, our gardener, sat smiling outside his hut on a box, with a mouthful of black stumps and a big flat loaf filled with sardines. He couldn't speak English and was seldom seen gardening. He kept snails in a nearby enclosure, and took them home to eat every now and then. The back door is standing open and the walls are thick and dusty. Our Maltese maids, Frances and Katy, chatter and giggle in the kitchen, and I hear their sandals flapping. The afternoon is hot and blue.

I am afraid here. This is not a hospital I am wet. Change me.

My Gozo hat crowded my forehead and my cotton frock plastered itself against me as I walked down the steps to the little orange tree garden. I was enclosed in its high stone walls and fixed within it like an embryo. Small, greenish oranges hung from the tree, and with a twitch of respect, I saw the snake on the ground in front of it. It was making unfamiliar, persuasive movements, as though it were possessed, and had no fancy of its own.

Watching it nailed me clean to the ground, until suddenly it cleared itself from its skin, seething away as bright as gold behind the tree, the skin a thin, brittle sash left on the ground. I stood, and then went and touched it, but it was nothing, like tissue paper. I gave a big jump back and went away in to tell my mother, who was stretching her eyes to put on mascara for a party. I told her, and I said I was bang near the snake, but that I had stood bang still. She said it was very exciting and that I was quite right to keep bang still.

I dragged upstairs into the great big nursery with the cool stone floor. My brother's snails oozed about in their compound, waiting for someone to discover them. He moved them to a different place each day, singing German lullabies to them.

Since there was no one there to ask, I helped myself to barley water from the pitcher and sat down at the table. The night nurseries opened off the day nursery, and in one slept my blameless youngest brother.

I felt a prime shiver of power as I bent over him. His curled hands were thrown back over his head and his eyelashes lay sweetly upon his cheeks like arcs, everything a little misty with sweat, as undefended as we all are in sleep. It wasn't much trouble to put my hand between the bars of the cot and give him a neat pinch. It wasn't enough to make him yell, but he thumped his fist about, and gave a turn and breathed and moaned and gave a chirk and suddenly, wham down again asleep. And I ran back into the day nursery, first looking to see if the tiger had got off the top of my mosquito net and was charging me.

He wasn't. And my mother always said there was no tiger, anyway. I had seen him though, licking his paws and waiting to jump out on to me.

I went downstairs to tell my father about my snake, and told him I was still worried about the tiger on my mosquito net. He said I must try not to worry, there wasn't really one, it was just a shadow I could see up there. Would I like to read a play with him, he said.

I couldn't answer, because a kind of fear pinioned me, and I said: 'Will you and Mummy always be here? Sometimes I feel afraid, as though something may happen. Are you sure you'll be here?'

He said everyone had those feelings, and of course they would always be there. I said I wished they weren't going out that night, and yes, I would like to read a play with my father, who in his spare time directed at the Princess Theatre in nearby Floriana, where I had long planned a standing ovation for myself. The fuss inside me had begun to move away already. It was cooler, too, and I went outside on to the terrace and stood looking up through the vines, and I called in to my parents: 'I think Malta is my favourite – even with the boys here. Don't you? Let's stay here forever. Don't you think?'

And by the next day my inner tumult had filtered away, and our afternoon rest swaddled us in heat and safety until the sleeping household unfolded. Till then, time sprawled ahead and away beyond reckoning, and we dreamed we were grown up, and perhaps answering questions instead of asking them. Needles of light threaded through the room from the dark green shutters, hot against the darkness.

And I opened my eyes and looked at my arm, as tough as a withy, the bubble of sweat in the hollow of my elbow ready for licking, which I did.

Upon the floor my sandals lay, ruthlessly entangled, as though some skirmish had overtaken them. The boys lay splayed on their beds, as lumpish as boulders, and, trapped on each of our nets, whined one scrupulous mosquito, blood–sated yet still thirsting.

I thought, oh, I am necessary to the green sea water, I am immediate and must touch the end of the world beneath it, and will bring back a sea horse.

I listened to the Maltese women and children shouting outside and imitated them meticulously, automatically boxing the recall in case it should be useful. I padded out of bed and pushed the shutters open, leaning on the sill, and under the pepper tree I saw our mongrel lift his profligate's head and bark, wait for a street dog's echo, and settle it again upon his hot paws, moving his dry tongue. 'Lazy!' I called. 'Your water's in the hall.' In the silent house, the house felled with sleep, I went downstairs and filled his bowl, and said again, 'Lazy!', as I went up to the nursery and our bedrooms.

Donkeys brayed a thick unorthodox yell, and I saw a herd of goats patter along the road like rain, and bleat like infants in the lagging afternoon, waiting before each doorway to give milk. Except English doorways, for the English might not drink Maltese goats' milk, or they would certainly contract Malta fever. The English therefore desisted, and caught the usual maladies, while the Maltese drank only goats' milk and remained radiantly healthy and a deal more charming. Perhaps it is worth adding that the goats lived on a diet of garbage, and that since there were only three cows on the island, and their milk was for the consumption of the Governor, we all had tinned milk, which we enoyed very much.

I heard the creak of Nanny's bed in her room next door as she put her feet to the floor and clicked her belt, clearing her throat to cover the sound. I suppose she thought it might inflame some passing goat boy. Anyway, she went clacking off to the kitchen for a cup of tea. You could always tell it was her, because she thought sandals were debauched, and wore grey lisle stockings and hard little black strap shoes that you could hear down every one of the stone steps. If it hadn't been for our baby brother, she would never have come out with us – it was far too hot, and she wore the full Kensington Gardens get-up most of every day. She never swam because that was for children, and as far as company was concerned, there were only about two other proper nannies in Sliema and one of them wasn't English, so she could be discounted at once. And she could hardly talk to Frances and Katy, our maids, because they couldn't speak English, and worse still, wore the faldetta, which was foreign.

On the whole, she didn't mind the food because it

was usually English, but carped at the way in which it was prepared, taking disapproving breaths and pushing it round her plate. She thought the Maltese people were immoral and dirty, no doubt because the little boys peed in the streets, which we thought both skilled and elegant and she thought ill-judged if not menacing.

No one knew where Nanny went on her day off, but one day she asked my mother's permission to take me with her, and I went, wearing rather tidier clothes than usual, and my better, though not best, sandals. I also wore my topee, since Nanny always thought it rather classy. She wore a long-sleeved white blouse, a long white skirt, those black shoes, and a rather thin wavy Panama hat. A striped shopping bag carried a Thermos of tea, some ginger nuts, and a bottle of lemon barley water. In a piece of pink material was her pink knitting.

And we walked down Strada Ghar-i-dud where our house was, and waited for a bus. Since I knew she had never cared for me very much, I rather wondered at this expedition, and stood kicking at the fragile dust, which spun about in the air.

A little rattling bus picked us up and bucked and lobbed us about a good deal. We didn't talk much, and Nanny hardly answered when I asked where we were going, but simply asked me whether I was being a good girl, and I said I was, and looked out of the window at the waxen countryside.

We got off the bus at a small village with a white square and a snatch of low stone houses. Goats consumed brown paper with the disinterest of courtesans, and a donkey stood immobile under a tree, like tourist pottery. And the blessed tug of brotherhood kept the village entire, the men prating, the women making lace, and laughing and looking. Though they only looked at me, since they seemed to know Nanny well enough to exchange nods with her. She smiled at them and then back at me, in a particular way, quite proudly, because she knew I was watching and hoped that I was aware that these people were her friends. Yet her manner was not greatly familiar with them, for in my presence she must indicate that they had not the standards expected in any nursery of hers. She was, in fact, making certain of her position in front of me.

It was, however, clear upon this bright, sluggish afternoon, with the animals lacklustre and dry and Turkish delight in the offing, that such false values might be waived. And it was for Turkish delight that we went to the only little shop there, since chocolate and ice cream contained goats' milk and thus were not allowed. Nanny said, 'Come along, you can carry the bag,' and I came along and carried the bag, and her black distorted shoes clacked along in front of me to the shop.

It was dark and heavy inside and there was a statuette of the Virgin on a little shelf, and a bale of black cotton at one end of the raw counter. The smell of haberdashery and bread, and perhaps sardines, panted through from a room at the back, and the sun clouted us as we came out with Turkish delight for both of us, and a piece of Maltese lace for me.

I felt pale with heat and devoured by my topee as we walked across the square. The goats shifted here and there with a pock-pock sound, some of them with a child's little arid cough, settling again like a bunch of twigs.

We found a seat and sat down, and I took off my topee, my hair stamped against my scalp. Nanny said: 'Put it on again,' and I did, runnels of sweat tickling my face. She took out the Thermos, the ginger nuts and the Turkish delight, and gave me the barley water. I said was this our tea, and she nodded and gave me a ginger nut. I felt suddenly sorry for her, for the first time. I think it was the ginger nuts and the way she wasn't saying anything. I put my hand on hers, and she moved it away – not crossly, but as though she wanted me to be careful what I said.

We had a few ginger nuts each, and Nanny drank all the tea and I had half the barley water. I put the Turkish delight on a piece of paper, as though it was for a party. And I said: 'Do you always come here on your half-day?'

After she'd wiped her mouth, she started to pack everything away, and then she said: 'I come here if and when I am asked. I never go where I'm not asked, it isn't good manners, you know that as well as I do. If there's nowhere to go, then I don't go anywhere. Do up your sandals and wipe your face, it's time we were off. David'll be needing his bath soon and it would never do to be late for that, now, would it?'

On the way back, when we were thumping about in the bus, she said I'd been quite a good girl, and that she was pleased with me. I thanked her, and when we got home my mother said to me: 'Well, darling, I think it's quite simple – she wanted to show you off to her friends, and to show them off to you. After all, she doesn't have much fun over here – it's not like going to see her sister in Croydon, is it? You must try and use your imagination a bit more.' And the world turned, with it our unaccented childhood, blessed and garrisoned and gloriously certain of a scant hour of morning school, and afternoons spent in the green chuck of sea round Malta. You could see clear to the bottom, sea urchins waiting to spindle you, sea anemones tensely delaying defloration with that sudden virginal contraction.

A few weeks after my excursion with Nanny, I contracted some malady and was put to bed, weak, aching and sticky, and with mosquitoes twanging round my room. Only when I had ceased to feel a red–hot steel band round my forehead was I assumed to be a little better, and after a week I was allowed in my wheelchair under the pepper tree to start my convalescence.

Unfortunately, I was not quite well enough to see Noël Coward when he came to dinner, and therefore handed my father a note beforehand, stating that since I was talented, pretty, and possessed of an extremely nice lizard, perhaps I could have an audience with Mr Coward. Had I known then that my father had turned down an actor called David Niven for a job with the Malta Amateur Dramatic Society, I might have added that in as well. As it was, my efforts carried no weight, and my parents suggested I look out of my bedroom window and see all three of them sitting on the terrace having an amusing conversation before dinner. I did so, with the certain knowledge that the dinner prepared for Mr Coward would be less than alluring, and that depending upon the time he had spent in Malta, he would undoubtedly expect this.

At that time, the food on the island fell into two equally hazardous categories, the first being the folly of eating Maltese food, unless you happened to be Maltese yourself. Should a Britisher make the ultimate error of sitting down to platefuls of squid and the sort of vegetables we all know are unnecessary, then he would certainly take a fever and die.

This might well be preferred to the second alternative.

Our Maltese maids, the Gauci sisters, sweet, well-meaning, and stifling their laughter, would choose some delicacy from an English cookery book, and Mr Coward would be presented with steamed fish and white sauce with mashed potatoes, and raspberry blancmange, garnished with tinned pears.

And he would eat it, and like it, and had probably become accustomed to it. For it was good nursery food, and everyone seemed to eat it at that time. All that messed-about stuff that you see these days wouldn't have been touched, then.

From Malta, most wonderfully remembered, was Frances's chocolate cake baked lovingly in the small cool kitchen in our house in Strada Ghar-i-dud. And it was remembered when we were at home in icy wartime England. I remember, too, the lace lady who called with a basket of Maltese lace to sell, and patted my cheek and said she had a little girl like me. She gave me a lace butterfly or rose, and pulled her faldetta together, smiling. My mother never bought any lace. She didn't like it. But the lace lady came regularly. She always smiled, and if the lace basket was very full, she let me choose a little piece. Then I thanked her and we smiled. She hardly spoke any English. But she often said that about having a little girl just like me, so once I asked her to bring the little girl next time, so that I could play with her. She didn't, though.

Frances's chocolate cake, dark and damp and as sharp as a cocoa bean, was not made from any recipe, but from the sinew of Frances's background and memory, succulent, a little lopsided, the icing soft and thick but not level, not seen to. And her sister, Katy, set it down in the drawing room, saying: 'Mind you don't shall touch till your Mummy come.'

I stood on the stone floor of the drawing room in cotton shorts and a white shirt looking at the cake, and I felt a strangeness in me that I could not account for. As though I only had to look behind me to discover the extra bits of knowledge that I needed to fit everything together. And I felt I had been standing on that spot since some of me was born, and I thought, I must get back. But I didn't know what I meant or where I had to get to.

The poppy-scarlet blood is grossly stopped, my life disqualified and fallen away for eighteen years.

My mother came in through the French windows, and the sun splashed on her through the vines outside. Everything packed together in me, and she said, 'You are getting tall, aren't you? Oh, chocolate cake, how wonderful. What are we going to do without it when we go back to England? Call the others.'

Years later, in Wiltshire, during the war, we looked out of the windows at the fog cuffing at the panes and checked the blackout, wondering what might take us from the night sky suddenly, the country sky. No sirens yet – I am on my leave, my Red Cross uniform put away. This house is far too big.

I thought, it's cold for lambing, and heard the first siren and my mother saying, 'Darling. Do you remember Frances's chocolate cake?' The mound of dogs querulously stirred in front of the fire as we picked burrs off them and remembered Frances's chocolate cake.

In Malta we swim before breakfast, just us, my father and I. The feverish sea anemones are blessed and chaperoned by the shelving rocks of Tigne and we are stowaways in the quartz-green sea. My father says I am a good strong swimmer and I am beyond Nanny and the boys and the white buckskin shoes I wear for parties and the awful tortoiseshell slide I wear every day, for now I will always be a strong swimmer.

We drive home and in the car I ask him: 'What would you like me to be like when I am completely grown up?'

'Well, I would hate you to be a bore,' he said. 'No one clears a room quite so quickly as a bore. And think about other people.'

We did not talk for a few moments, then he said: 'You see, I want you to be happy, but not at other people's expense. Think how lovely everything will be when you are married.'

I was aghast and said nothing. A flock of goats crossed in front of the car, the call of their bells languid and fitful. I said nothing, nothing until we got home to Islay House. Then, in case he should say any more about being married, I said: 'Could you come and have breakfast with me in the nursery?'

But he couldn't, because his was already laid on the terrace under the curling vines and brindled shade that eased the morning's heat.

I stood, watching him settle, and the air moved lightly round us in the shallows of the day.

'Would you like some of our barley water from the nursery?' I said.

He said it was exactly what he would like. He said that although there was already barley water on the table, he felt that the nursery barley water would be more sustaining. On the one hand he talked to me as though I were a child, and on the other he talked of marriage.

77

I felt the indignity of each as I went up to the nursery for the barley water. There were two pieces of bread and butter covered with muslin on the table. I stuffed one into my mouth and thought, I am a slave. I eat leftovers. Nobody cares about me.

I carried the heavy earthenware jug down the uneven stone stairs and carefully on to the terrace. With my mouth full, I poured some barley water for my father and sat down at the other side of the table, praying that Nanny wouldn't come down to see why there was only one slice of bread on the nursery table.

'What about your breakfast?' asked my father.

'Just swallowed it,' I said, almost choking to death. 'I wanted to get back quickly in case you needed me.'

He stroked my hand and said, 'Don't be too much of a handmaiden, darling.'

After a reasonable silence, I said, 'When you've finished, could we play words and colours?'

It was quite a simple game. We often played it, and my mother was very good at it. One of you said a word and suggested a colour the word might be. Everybody else disagreed and shouted and put forward their own ideas. There were no winners but a lot of argument and my mother and father said it stretched the imagination.

My father finished his breakfast and lit a cigarette before starting with the first word. It was 'Peru', he said, and it was dark purple. I said it should be a kind of burnt orange, that purple was too heavy, but he said I was wrong. The next one he said was 'knitting', and the colour, off-white. It seemed fair and I allowed it.

But in my head came a word, a name darker, more beautiful and more unscrupulous than any I knew. I felt it sharp as the cut of a crystal.

'Gandolfini,' I said. 'Gold and black.'

'Where did it come from?' said my father.

I said, 'It was in my ear. I heard it. And I heard the colours. Gold. And black.' I did not tell anyone that when I heard the colours, I saw a leopard.

Although my father had a deal of work to do since he was then Assistant Military Secretary to Sir John du Cane, the Governor of Malta, a span of indolence spread across our days for much of the time. Often, my mother lay for hours in the drawing room, shutters defending its undersea stillness until she woke, and beneath our mosquito nets we stirred from our rests to the sound of the gramophone and Edith Piaf's tortured keening.

Sometimes, in the afternoons, we watched my father play polo at the Marsa, the boiling tornado of horses and dust pleasing and disturbing me, the sweat and glory of our heroes calling up the tainted violence of the playing field.

Once I grabbed a small girl standing next to me and said: 'That's my father, the fastest one, the one with the nicest topee, you can see he's the best, can't you?' And I added, 'The other one – that's Mountbatten. You can see he's not much good, poor thing, I feel quite sorry for him.' I would have been happier if I could have referred to him as 'Dicky', which was what my father called him, but we were never allowed to Christian-name grown-ups of course.

'You were the best,' I said when my father came up.

My last childhood illness hit me when we arrived back in England, and, with great courage, Katy came over to nurse me. Like most young Maltese women, she had seldom even left her village, quite apart from her country, yet shy, nervous and devoutly Roman Catho-lic, Katy got a boat, and three weeks later walked down the gangplank in her faldetta, with her crucifix, rosary, and a small china Madonna for me, with messages from Frances and a new shiny holdall. And this remarkable sight was never forgotten by my parents. It was an undertaking that needed considerable resolution from such a young woman, particularly since she had little English and felt that if a Catholic church did not present itself within moments of her arrival, then she must go straight back to Malta, however much she loved us all.

But all was well, and she was treasured. Out of doors, she wore the faldetta which was in any case a badge of modesty, but did, of course, attract some attention, causing her to return weeping at the way she was being looked at, and not, she sobbed, only by young women.

Thus, within a week, she was wearing eau-de-nil rayon blouses, although she still wore her full black skirt. The faldetta was put away for her return, and she cheered up considerably, only weeping if young men looked at her.

And she fed me, washed me, chattered, giggled and played games with me, and when I got better she went back to Malta in tears, as we all were. We didn't see her again. Each Christmas, highly coloured cards of the Virgin and Child arrived from her and Frances, with, written inside: 'Please Madam and Colonel with children is Happy Christmas Wish you shall to come back. Our Lord take care you.'

But we never went back, because the war wrenched Malta and England apart, and I was sent to a kind of finishing-stroke-domestic school in Dorset for the daughters of gentlemen.

In the meantime, I had to contend with the bruiser that was adolescence. I felt I ought to be treated as a grown-up, but my looks were hardly alluring and thus knocked such a wish on the head, for I was as thin as a thread, as pale as junket and my eyebrows, like twin black caterpillars, tramped across my brow, meeting to squabble over my nose, while sullen breakers of hair partly obscured my face. An effort to emulate Lorna Doone by skilful shaping with my mother's nail scissors merely resulted in a more than glancing likeness to Ben Gunn.

Worst of all were my clothes which, almost outgrown, fought and wrangled round my body as though trying to escape. And, lamentably, I still wore my brother's grey shorts and Aertex shirts. I wept quite often, but quietly.

Miss Alexander, whose responsibility I had remained, always treated my vapourings with austere affection, deplorable though she must have felt my outward appearance to be. It was only when I came down to breakfast for the fifth day running wearing the usual tattered shorts that she said, 'Save us, child, have you nothing else to wear?'

She was much given to such a form of speech, reminiscent as it was of one of Sherlock Holmes's housekeepers, and I loved her for it, but just now I needed approbation and said, 'Am I in the least pretty?'

She touched my cheek and said, 'You have a very interesting face, my dear.'

But I didn't want an interesting face, I wanted beauty, admiration, to turn heads. Every morning I prayed to be beautiful, and each morning I awoke not beautiful. Who would ever watch me pass and say: 'There goes a beautiful grown-up'?

In a state of flux, I went and sat on a box in the

garage. What was needed was a list of things to do that might further the cause of beauty. I wrote:

1. Try Eating Flowers to Clean Out My Inside.
2. Wash Face With Rainwater From Water Butt To Get Skin Better.
3. Wash Hair With Saved Breakfast Egg And Rinse With Vinegar.
4. Clean Nails More Often (With Vim) And Try Not To Bite Them.

The flowers I attempted to eat were campion, shepherd's purse and pimpernel, fidgeted forth from the cracks in paving, and the result was not so much beautifying as purging, nor did it taste too good either. I washed my face with rainwater only once, deterred from experimenting further by the amount of small insects floating on the water's surface. The tips of my fingers stung when I cleaned my nails with Vim so I didn't use it again, but the thin sweetness of a cloverhead, when sucked, honeyed my disposition, thus making amends. And the breakfast egg proved too difficult to save without discovery, so I ate it for breakfast the day after I had tried to save it. Overnight it lay under the bath together with *Forever Amber* and I smuggled it down to the dining room the next day. By then it didn't taste very nice, and I was glad to see the back of it.

I had a frock specially made for me when my parents took me to Ascot, and my hat was quite expensive and so were my shoes. My father had written a poem for me called 'A Modern Girl', so I was very nearly grown up.

But I felt alone suddenly. There was a standing-still of everything, a lack of tempo, an alteration in the direction of my living and some little change in me, felt but not seen. Inside me was a black shadow like the black velvet brushstroke in a scarlet poppy's petal.

My parents were talking to some friends. My mother turned towards me and said something and I answered: 'No, I'm perfectly all right, thank you,' and so I was. Perfectly. And in any case we would soon be going to the Eton and Winchester match.

It was hot that day and I wore the same frock and a different hat so that I still felt fairly grown up, and one or two people looked at me, which I enoyed.

The marquee where we had strawberries and cream shimmered in the heat, and in front of the entrance stood three Indian ladies hardly moving, their saris of brilliant breathless colours – tangerine, caramel and a plunging damson. They turned their heads a little this way and a little that, speaking to each other in light skimming voices, perhaps in Urdu. Their hands curled like freesias, and sometimes a catching of the sun made their jewels glance and take fire as they turned.

I enjoyed these excursions which were the beginning of my grown-up life. But I could not help noticing that there was something sadly lacking in my physical development. It was breasts. I was not yet eligible for a bra, then called a bust-bodice and generally made in a colour called tea rose, though I sometimes looked at them in shop windows and gave desperate prayerful sighs for proper grown-up breasts. Breasts lent one a certain flourish, an éclat, but the slightness of my buds took from me the little dignity I had, somehow slowing down my growing up.

Nonetheless, at a party where everyone but I had breasts, someone tried to kiss me and I ran away and wept and said, 'You mustn't do that, I don't like it, and I don't think our dogs would like me to do it either,' and cried because I felt the turning wheel again, a change, a difference and myself afraid. And yet I wished that he might do it again, the wheel of birds in my plain, dependable mind, and I have a pain Mummy, I have a pain I have a pain and I think, but I am not sure, that I would like him to do it again. I want everything to be as it was when I was a little girl. I don't want to be grown up after all, and I cried for the destruction of my hopes and the fear prickling my nape so suddenly. And I wondered if I would ever see him again.

I did not. Nor did I tell my mother anything at all. For I believe that what I wanted was to fall, as true as a plumb line, in love with somebody who loved me, and to be hopelessly and lovingly trapped, bumping into people, stammering, and perfectly blurred with it. But of course there mustn't be any kissing. None. None whatsoever.

Autumn consumed summer, slicing, paring and narrowing itself to the day when my parents would drive me to Harcombe House for domestication and finish. But before that, two things happened to me. First I failed to make face cream out of mashed-up rose petals and lard, and next was something quite new and grown up.

When I saw the blood, I knew at once that it was what my mother had talked about, so I wasn't frightened. We were in London at the time, at Eccleston Square, and I walked up about five flights of stairs to her room where she sat writing letters at the bureau. I said: 'Did you think I was someone coming up with a delicious cup of tea? Or some thin bread and butter?'

She said: 'Yes, in a way I did, but I'm glad it's you instead. What is it, darling?'

'Blood is what it is,' I said. 'Like you told me and you said to come and tell you, so here I am.'

She kissed me and made a lovely fuss over me, putting me on her bed under the eiderdown while she found an ST for me, so that I began to feel extremely grand and clever. The holly berry in the carol came into my head. '*As red as any blood* . . .' I thought.

'Will I go on having it until I'm old?' I asked.

She said: 'Well, not old exactly. It'll go on until the middle of your life probably, although occasionally a bad shock may stop it. No need for either of us to worry about that, I imagine.'

Nonetheless, her menstruation was to stop from shock when my father died in 1940, and mine stopped in 1969, also from shock and from the splinter that turned in my mind and turning, changed me.

But that late afternoon in London, I left my mother's room with muted self-importance, not to say arrogance.

Harcombe House was run by a Mrs Francillon, bony and formidable in ankle-length black, a choker and with a foam of white hair. Largely unapproachable, she would walk with measured step through kitchen, sewing room and laundry (which she pronounced lahn-dry), commenting positively upon our pintucks and French seams and our tenderness in crystallising violet petals for exquisitely handmade chocolates. It was said that mayonnaise curdled at her step, while a separation of syllabub was not unknown. And it was thought that she might be a witch, and that her familiars were her two little griffons that sometimes nested in her skirts. Their very names, Pippin and Fancy, had something of an arcane quality.

But we liked her, though we shrank against the walls

as she tapped down corridors and up stairs, occasionally turning to sharply call the little dogs to her.

And Harcombe was quite pleasant, although I did not feel I would ever get on to the stage, what with it and the war.

It was full of girls whose eyebrows did not join blackly across their noses like mine did. And I did not have a thing called an afternoon frock like the others, and wrote to my mother, 'Darling Mummy, I do not have a thing called an afternoon frock. Apparently nothing else will do. What will they do to me? And what is it anyway?'

She wrote: 'Fortnums are sending you two on approval. You could send one back if you hate it. Or both if they're frightful. Are you enjoying it?'

I wrote: 'No, I can't say I'm enjoying it yet. They got a bit cross because I forgot to put the flour in my Victoria Sponge.'

Whilst my afternoon frocks could hardly be called dashing, modelled as they were on Deanna Durbin's wardrobe, yet they were not unbecoming, and I began to be aware of an amelioration in my looks, which, however, could hardly be confused with anything so flagrant as beauty.

I wrote to my mother: 'I think my skin's better, and I wish I had some decent clothes. My hair doesn't really look like proper hair, whatever I do with it. Next time you go to your man, could I come too?'

She wrote: 'Darling, don't have your hair done by Vasco – he always makes one look like the Apollo Belvedere. I daren't even have tea at the Club until I've spent five minutes in a lift somewhere, pulling it all to pieces. Clothes, well, I don't really know. The war's going to make that kind of thing difficult. We'll see.'

What I really wanted to ask her was whether she thought I was going to turn out to be the kind of girl anyone could fall in love with, but we weren't on those sort of terms, and it would have meant a lot of side-stepping, so I didn't.

I left the school without a diploma, but with a reprimand for having organised a midnight feast, and the threat of expulsion for smoking during my first term.

They taught me the right way to make white cotton knickers, and how to write out a cheque, which last proved more than satisfactory for the rest of my life. And when I came home, I went to stay with my Aunt Barbara at her studio in Chelsea, and the distinction of having a sculptor for an aunt still gives me a helluva shout inside. I had plenty of boundaries pushed away from my vision, and she exercised my perceptions so early in my life that I began lapping up fresh persuasions sooner than most girls.

But the most enoyable brouhaha was always caused by the great tree that grew up through the floor of the studio, and away up through the roof, for the Press to photograph and exclaim over, and for me to show off to sightseers. I don't go to Chelsea now, and know the formal dying that I felt, but could not fetch up so long ago.

When I was a student, the sooty glamour of London pleasantly disturbed the measure of my thoughts, but now, the King's Road, where we bought bread, and second-hand picture frames, has taken a sickly vulgarity which may attract the passer-by, but not us who still like our vulgarity rough and amiable.

Some of Barbara's sculpture, and young pinafored

photographs I have, and memories of Mrs Corner, well-meaning and disastrous on the days she came to clean, unfurling her black coat with a kind of startled chagrin, as though suddenly snapped at. But she knew her value, and that she was loved by the entire enclave of studios, and, jaws chopping, it was her pleasure queasily to drag a duster over everything, her eyes blank and absorbed.

I did the best kind of growing up at the studio. Pushed, rattled, peppered, extracted, implanted, told, explained and commended, I enjoyed and remember it all with a fierce sadness. I had the run of Barbara's books while she worked, studying with the attention of a child whose reading is never superintended. And since then, I have always expected it to be as enjoyable as that fizz of excitement that informed my senses in the studio.

Since I had early teethed upon my father's book of eighteenth-century French erotica, I discarded hers, and seeking more stringent pastures, came upon a book of mathematics, whose style and elegance evoked for me some sort of undiscovered glory even whilst most was enigmatic stuff.

But it lifted my heart to sit on the floor and read of Leonardo of Pisa, called Fibonacci, a twelfth-century mathematician, whose disarming number sequence even I could understand. I imagined him, particularly lean, and extra dark, and still blest with preoccupation, sitting in a shaded square in Pisa. Perhaps a little dog at his feet – Bruno, he calls it – and perhaps at his elbow lambent grapes lie and roll, and offer themselves. And so he takes one or two, and notices how the fig tree's complex roots lift the corner of the flagstones. The sun burns, and this logarithmic fellow, cloaked and tunicked, and with a little crack of absurdity about him, shoulders equations from him and swaggers off with ridiculous coxcombry into the Golden Ratio of Antique Pisa's afternoon.

I rediscovered Fibonacci and his number sequence in my fifties and was charmed again, and still add up on my fingers. Yet I am still aware of the dignity of numbers, and the fun.

From Barbara I remember the heady exoticism of the Ballet Russe de Monte Carlo, to which she introduced me when I was young, and which painted my life with remarkable glamour, for I not only saw the ballets with her at Covent Garden, but many of the dancers were her friends or models, and brought to the studio a nutshell smallness and muscularity and whispers of waspish dressing-room tiffs and wretchedness, too untidy to conceal. I learned of Taglioni, Camargo, Diaghilev and Nijinsky, and saw Tourmanova and Massine dance my first *Petrouchka* with her. And when the little rags of snow dropped over St Petersburg, Petrouchka's terrible death-cry stopped my heart, and I felt a tightening and a shaking and a sudden understanding that had to do with love and with death. And I embraced it, because it seemed that the two halves of me had come together, and that my centre was plumb, and would always be so.

I never asked Barbara about that feeling, but maybe I had discovered something she had done already, so I didn't try, but watched her in the restaurant afterwards as she ordered in quick and expert Italian, and felt extremely proud of her. There was so much to enjoy in her rather different world, that I never can lose. She was designing a ballet theatre commissioned for Broadway by Sol Hurok when she died – from cancer – the dispatch agonising and slow, and I was not there because it was in the fifties and I was working. She rang me from the hospital, and after that I did not see her again.

But I remember her in 1938, the sharp, dark smell of coffee coming through the studio door, and her sitting outside with a cigarette, taking a break and talking to friends, photographing and sometimes drawing me, encouraging me to plague the intractable cool clay and make of it some excitement.

Like a spider's web over a pile of rocks, the war was making little contact with many of us, and it hadn't yet begun to shave bits away from people's lives. So in order to feel necessary to one another, everyone went to a great many parties and dances, and drove to race meetings and cricket matches and picnics, and the telephone rang a good deal and it was often someone called Gerald or Adrian. If it wasn't, my mother put the receiver down, and said: 'Persona non grata, one may assume.'

None of it was really my cup of tea, and if I came home rather late, my mother questioned me minutely, chattering with nerves as she put *The Warden* down on her bedside table. I said of course he hadn't, didn't, wasn't, and kissed her goodnight. It was true. I was much too frightened to let anyone do anything. On the other hand, somehow I didn't really want to give the impression that I hadn't, because it made me seem so ingenuous.

No one believed the war would last longer than six months, and we moved to the nine-bedroomed house that my father had designed and had built for us, and sat about in more acres of ground than we had ever had before and asked people to stay, and the dogs of war put up pheasants that whirred and chunnered and batted away up through the trees. We said to each other how lovely it was, and what a lot of room, and our voices coiled up into the blank air like smoke.

The Defence of Calais took place in 1940, and at 3.30 p.m. on May 25th my father, Chandos Benedict Arden Hoskyns, was fatally wounded and brought back to a hospital in Winchester.

Everyone went to Winchester except me and my governess, Miss Alexander. The bulletins were encouraging, but it did not seem as though my father could possibly be back by my eighteenth birthday.

I went into my mother's bedroom and helped myself to one of her blouses. She hadn't said I couldn't, and I would tell her when she came home. I joined Miss Alexander for breakfast in the dining room. It was June 19th, and the sun slammed through the windows with such a collision of light that you had to look along a length of darkness before you could make any sense. The dogs panted outside the French windows and I let them in.

Miss Alexander took a cup of coffee and went to ring the hospital, and came back and didn't say anything. So I didn't either. Then she said: 'Well, it doesn't sound bad, darling. They'll ring in any case, so don't worry, there's nothing useful we can do here. Find yourself something to do, that's the best thing. Is that your mother's blouse? Well, don't get it dirty, will you?'

She went into the kitchen and I heard her saying: 'Well, it looks as though the Colonel's not doing too badly, thank goodness. We must make certain he gets some really good food when he gets home. If there's anything more, we'll soon know.' And she said she would be going into Salisbury by the next bus.

She said goodbye, and I sat in the garden on the

stepped lawn by the cypresses that were only a few feet high then. There were wood pigeons, and later in the year you could see the nests of rooks in the tops of trees and the keen tangle of ice on the grass.

I would go down to the post office for a Mars bar and some writing paper, and would write a poem for when my father came home. I might buy a packet of cigarettes to see what that was like.

I shut the dogs in the downstairs lavatory and went out.

You could see a bit of the village from the top of the drive, and it looked stooped and plump, but when you got down to the bottom, you could see the grand houses on one side, and the cottages, the shop and the church on the other, with the pub, the unexceptional stream and the bridges.

I saw someone coming towards me from the end of the drive, and we walked towards each other until I could see it was Mr McGowan, the vicar. I hardly knew him. He had a slight stammer, and often appeared somewhat uncomfortable, and this time he did not speak or smile. He stopped suddenly, outlined like a scarecrow by the sky and fields. I stopped too, but I said nothing.

I felt sick, because I knew what he was going to say, and I felt a sort of concentration, a distilment of myself. I waited. The dogs started barking. There was quite a long pause, and I wished he didn't have to say what he was there to say. Eventually, he said quickly: 'I'm sorry, my dear, I'm afraid – afraid that your father has—.' He took a long time with the next bit because he couldn't decide whether to say 'died' or 'passed away', and eventually he said 'passed away'. I didn't say anything, so he added: 'I'm very sorry', and I said, 'I see', and, 'Thank you'.

He asked if there was anything he could do, and I said no, thank you, that I was all right.

I watched him go down the drive. I should have offered him a cup of coffee, I suppose. I wondered what would happen to the polo ponies now. The dogs were going mad, so I let them out.

I didn't know what to do. I went and sat in the drawing room and felt as though someone else were inhabiting my skin and ordering my life and movements. I felt cold, and I went upstairs and was sick a little, and lay on my bed. There was no question of having a good cry because Daughters of the Regiment must show a form of bravery always, and by the time my governess had come back, somehow I had rearranged myself and was able to face things. For me, then, there was a certain healing, but it was slow, and my mother never recovered from my father's death. The show that some observed was not a quickening, but cloaked a still terrible unhappiness, and only helped her to face the otherness of others. She seldom spoke of my father, guarding herself from our beggarly attempts at comfort, for we were raw and maladroit. At eighteen I was the eldest and perhaps caught her grief more easily and painfully than my brothers, mostly away at school. But death being strange to me, I foundered upon my own wretchedness, and my mother became a displaced person, no country being hers, who could not even come to the funeral, but lay weeping in my grandmother's spare room.

Looking at my father's regimental cap and sword upon the coffin in Winchester Cathedral, I felt inside me a charge, sudden and inexplicable, like some flame, and began to cry, but fiercely stopped. I was glad my mother was not there, because I felt weakened.

Things did change a bit, as they did for everyone, and for me the changes were important and infinitesimal – I did not ride so often, nor did I draw to any useful degree, nor write, since my father had been an exemplar. Often I just sat remembering how he had taken me over my first jump. He seemed to be the guardian of people, just ordinary people with their majestic possibilities, and said they were not shabby till they were treated so. And even then, that it was only like a dog snapping. And that they must be kept warm, as it were, and listened to.

Two years before this I had leaned against my father's peacetime flannel knees in the Wiltshire garden. Barred and cross-barred, the shadow of an aeroplane shifted upon the lawn and hunt balls and regimental dances lay ahead of me. Soon I would be grown up, but now I was sixteen.

'Gandolfini,' I said.

'What?' said my father, and slept.

I said 'Gandolfini' again and heard it in my head, a golden tremor, stealthy and godless as pleasure taken in Lent.

Hunt balls and regimental dances and young men standing too close to me and I don't want it, I don't want it.

But the beginning of the war had slammed its bolt, and my father was dead. I could not take or bear his death, and I kept his letters in an envelope.

Before the war, there was a difference. I lay on the striped new grass and leaned against my father and watched a hill of rail-roading ants in that sedated, warm and untried garden, as raw as a carpenter's bench, yet sided by fields and gates and spinneys and coppices, a stepped lawn and a cracking big kitchen garden.

During the run-up to the war, my life gently lay, put out for me with small chance of seeing its confines skewed, and each autumn was drummed out in unspent silences.

In one silence I stroked my father's knee and said, 'If I had a choice, I think I would like to marry you, but I suppose there's no chance of bending the law in that direction, is there?'

'None, darling,' my father said. 'You see Mummy would never allow it for one thing, and for another thing, how am I going to hand you up the aisle when you're a bride?'

I said, 'I hope you'll wear your sword when you hand me up the aisle. It'll add a bit of class.'

'I will if it's that sort of wedding,' he said.

'Will you be sad when you give me away?' I asked.

'Inconsolable, but my bravery will be remarked by all. Though of course Mummy will be the bride's mother and will be able to do all sorts of silly things and no one will mind a bit.'

On the warm grass, I spread and slept. When I woke I saw that the aeroplane's shadow had moved away.

I was still sixteen when I woke up and my mother and father were drinking sherry on the terrace. My bare feet were hot on the paving stones and I walked carefully on my heels.

I asked my mother whether I could wear pink on my wedding day. She said I could not wear pink nor blue nor custard nor eau-de-nil, but only white. She said I had to be a debutante before I became a bride. She said that the rule about weddings was that none of the guests could wear white for fear of eclipsing the bride. But, she said, the bride was usually so radiantly happy that no one could possibly eclipse her in any case.

But my father never handed me up the aisle because by then he had died, and the wedding took place at Kensington Register Office and I did not wear white.

Our war was Calais. The aeroplane's shadow lay barred and cross-barred on the grass and my father and I will lie against each other, cross on cross.

Inexorably, the war set in. Like a small blaze in an empty house, it could be almost overlooked to start with, consisting as it did of minor drawbacks, the blackout, form-filling, rations and making one's night-dresses out of butter muslin, dyed in a basin on the Aga. The words most likely to cause an affray were: 'No, Madam, I'm afraid we haven't any. It's the war, you see.' But we managed.

And it was desultory enough in the early months, before it seemed necessary for any of us to take on real war work.

In this context, I became secretary to the colonel of the local Home Guard, and stood about in tweeds and a Veronica Lake hairstyle, making incomprehensible lists and sometimes shrugging my shoulders. Eventually I was sacked because no one could read my lists, so I had a Tio Pepe with the Colonel, who was a friend of my mother's, and went home.

Next, I worked in a Forces Canteen and then packed Prisoner of War parcels before killing time with intensive singing lessons which revealed split vocal chords but quite a good voice. Mme Hubler, the pleasant martinet in charge of my singing lessons, also set me to translate the whole of *Cyrano de Bergerac* into English. Enthusing over my voice, but deploring my translation, she left to start a finishing school in Switzerland.

Every now and then, I went to a cocktail party and

once met Augustus John, who wanted to paint me and said so. Since I had not noticed him wanting to paint anyone else and was much taken with his cloak and huge hat, I sought out my mother in a kind of submerged turmoil.

I had hardly opened my mouth than she removed me to the far end of the room with the words, 'Certainly not, I forbid it. Surely you've heard about his reputation?' I said, 'But wouldn't you rather like me to hang in Burlington House?'

She said tartly there were other places to hang and other ways of doing it. I had to wait till I was in my thirties to hang in Burlington House. It was worse a few months later when I told her someone wanted to paint me in the nude. She took a step back and shrieked, 'Who?'

I said, 'Well, he's perfectly, I mean dispassionate, I mean objective, I mean not really interested in naked people. I mean, what he feels is that—' I trod on the dog and said, 'You may be interested to hear that he's married.' Even that was suspect. 'Why doesn't he paint his wife then?' said my mother.

I became a VAD, which was what I had wanted, and which doubtless would be called a Red Cross nurse today.

Some time was spent at first with a military tailor who told me how nice I was going to look, and that he had a niece who was a VAD, and she always looked very ladylike. 'It's the colour,' he said. 'That navy, you see. Very distinguished, if you know what I mean. Not like', he lowered his voice, 'the others.'

And he fixed me up, as he put it, with a dark blue

greatcoat, and coat and skirt reminding me that everything else, caps, frocks, aprons, came from an outfit-
ter's. And he waved me out, saying I mustn't forget the
shoes. 'Black,' he said. 'Nurse's. Standard. That's what
you ask for. When do you start?'

I told him, and he said: 'Well, good luck then. My
niece, Amy her name is, she loves it. Hard work she
says, and between you and me mucky too, but, well,
good luck anyway.'

The moment you put your uniform on, you are a
nurse. But when I walked on to the ward at the
Infirmary for a week's training before I was posted, all
the staff and every patient knew me for a rookie. My
apron was too clean, and my cap too starchy, and
everything I did seemed to upset the entire ward. No
one ever asked me if I knew how to do something. I
just did it and hoped to die. And I mustn't flag or be
sick or even sit down. I must not smile at the doctor.
This familiarity is Sister's prerogative.

It is forbidden to run, and it is forbidden to sit on the
patient's bed.

Don't fall over. If you do, the patients will lose faith
in you.

The sluice is for emptying bedpans. It is not a
smoking room.

Pale with apprehension, I knew that when Sister's
voice resounded through the ward thus: 'Where are all
my nurses? This isn't going to win the war,' what she
meant was, 'Is Nurse Hoskyns still rolling bandages?'

But when the course ended, I discovered I had learned
a great deal more than I thought, beginning with the
ability to walk down the ward, with a moderated step
and with composure. I learned to do as I was told, and
to get it right absolutely and immediately, and that I

98

was important in one degree only – that the amount of work, though overpowering, must be accomplished with the least possible discomfort to my patients, and without showing any distaste for what might be some markedly distasteful jobs. While I was not daunted, I did not appreciate the Herculean stamina needed for the job. Nor did I realise that although I was to be happier and more fulfilled than I could have imagined, I might often be asleep on my feet for days, and that home leave merely meant drinking a cup of tea and falling into bed for forty-eight hours.

Before leaving the Infirmary for my posting, I apologised to Sister for wearing my cloak inside out because I thought the scarlet looked so pretty. I don't think she really forgave me. I never did it again.

My yearly check for tuberculosis was clear, and a week or two later, confident and *soignée* in my uniform, I left for Ellwood Auxiliary Hospital, where I was to nurse members of the Armed Forces, just like in the movies. It was clear, as I stepped across the threshold and asked for Matron's office, that my stage career would not materialise for some years. I was further daunted by the sight of so many men sitting about in the hall chatting and laughing, some in plaster or on crutches and many of them actually smoking, with, I was glad to see, ashtrays. Some of these men, I was shocked to notice, were joking with the VADs – pretending to kiss them and so on. This was not quite what I had expected, and I decided I would allow no such thing, and went into Matron's office.

Nurses are the romantic clichés of all wars and many movies. We were up at 6.30 a.m. and off at 8 p.m. for £1 a week, looking like seraphs, working like hauliers. On night duty, cloaked and shivering, we did the ward rounds, and in the day tried to sleep through the dogged sunlight on the curtains. We were tired all the time. Only when we sat down, though.

We nursed all kinds of patients with all sorts of maladies, and it did none of us any harm. Mental patients came to us sometimes if beds were scarce elsewhere. Nursed as bed-patients sometimes, they were always accorded the security of communication and kindness. At that time, tablets were not leaned on to any great extent, and although few of us had ever heard of Professor Jung, instinctively we seemed to follow many of his precepts in addition to our own instructions.

A VD patient did not do too well with us socially, since Sister had to admit that for him to have caught gonorrhoea he must have been up to something she did not care to think about, far less envisage. Although, as one of us murmured, 'I shouldn't think she would know how to envisage it.' Matron, being more humane, was very nice to him, but the younger nurses were forbidden to go near him, and he was treated as a leper. I was a little older, and in any case was senior by then, and often went into his little isolation ward, warding off the possibility of Sister's corking severity and his confusion disconcerting one another.

In our romantic uniforms, and perhaps because of them, we learned to become a little more than the image smilingly suggested, and leaned no more than lightly into the elbowroom of this supposed repute, and in clean caps and aprons with their compassionate red crosses, we scrubbed floors, did dressings, disinfected screen castors, rolled bandages, swore when Sister wasn't there, flagged, drooped, panted for a cigarette, longed for a pee and wondered how long the 'duration' was going to be.

Dull, unthankful work, much of it was, redeemed by the affectionate sauce of our patients, who thought of us as angels and treated us so, never swearing in front of us, giving us their chocolate ration, blushing sometimes for the things we had to do for them, and often, desperately falling in love with us. They wrote to us afterwards sometimes, signing themselves, 'Yours, always, Corporal Clark, Nobby that cleaned the day room for you when the old battleaxe was out of the way. Remember?'

When we got this sort of thing, most of us would go into the loo and do some quick, neat crying before we came back wearing special faces. We were the nearest thing to security that they could conjure up, and Matron knew this, and smiled upon such innocences, considering them part of the therapy.

Ginger-haired and neat as a bird, I still hear the click of her shoes in the corridors. We were her nurses and she trusted us. If we defaulted, we were rebuked in private, with style and without taint of malice, and forgiven, dismissed and loved. 'I assure you, my nurses would be incapable of such conduct,' she pronounced when once our behaviour was questioned by a visiting VIP. Though later in her office, she called us to account.

The days were not ungifted, but the clemency of peacetime pulled away from us as we reached for it. We thought of simple things – enough chocolate, clothes without Utility labels, enough time to feel certain there would be more, enough to squander, to waste, lovely immoderate time.

I thought I need never plan again, and that I need never again feel anxious for other people's safety. And all of us were certain that the instant the war ended, we would fall in love with somebody reasonably good-looking and slightly rich, and get married. But I had to get to the RADA before anything else. We had been in uniform for too long.

In the staffroom, we lit cigarettes and read newspapers, listening to the wireless at tea-time before getting up and checking the time from the watches that were pinned to our blue frocks.

'You really wonder if it's going to end,' we said, nodding sagely, stubbing our cigarettes out in the shone-up brass ashtrays. One of us said: 'Who's taking Matron's tray up?' I was, and did so, checking that my apron was clean, and the tea tray as exactly laid as rationing allowed.

Matron's cap was on the dressing table, and her blue cape lay on the bed. Snowdrop, the white cat, was urged off her lap. Snowdrop and I had been on night-duty when the buzz bomb came over, I with my cloak and torch. The noise made me drop my torch, and Snowdrop took a flurry into the corner of the hall. Even senior nurses were permitted fear as long as patients were not privy to it.

When the war ended, it was slowly, like a breathless unwinding of nerves that still might pull too dangerously, and having felt them a little we flapped our expectations somewhat. But we never quite got back to the silly selves we had been before, and busily began work on the selves we felt we should become, but dandifying them rather.

So we all kissed each other, said we must meet again, but I think did not, and wished each other luck. We went home, and I packed away my uniform, was touched and pleased to be given an award, with others in the village, and felt inside me an expansion and an emotion, as though something had passed me that needed recognition, refused perhaps for lack of time. It was, I think, my father's death.

But busy with my dandified unregulated life, I made it clear to everyone that I was charming, intelligent and attractive by getting drunk at Churchill's and thus disgracing my brother; getting engaged to someone who tried to drown me; and yawning my way through Queen Charlotte's Ball and a cut-price photograph by Swaebe during the supper interval.

And I spent a year at a school of art, wasting my mother's money and eating doughnuts in the breaks. And I went to too many parties, dances and theatres, usually ending up asleep in the back of Gerald's, or Adrian's, or Nigel's car. Great and welcome pleasures.

I thought, the sooner I get out of all this and start doing the only thing I'm really interested in, the better.

Unimpeachable Cheyne Walk was where I lived while I was at the Royal Academy of Dramatic Art. Supreme also were Oakley Street and the King's Road, and the smell of the baker's shop in Milner Street. Trams made the whole room jar and jolt, and I fell out of bed each morning at dawn, trying to see my watch, my heart jumping, because the basement sounds that woke me had a hoarse grating and a descended threat behind them.

Boy-o, I saw you that first day at the Academy, I saw you. I saw you look at me and I saw my equilibrium leave me. I saw you and thought nothing of you, but like a hired assassin watched which way you went when the RADA spewed us out at the end of the day, and who you talked to when you were trying not to notice me. We were separate. If you sat at a particular table for lunch, I chose to sit at another. If we sat side by side in class, we pretended it was a mistake. My dear young man, my constant bright destruction, I have unmanageable feelings. As far as terms are concerned, these are mine: I will not settle for merely thinking about the dent in the back of your neck for the rest of my life, and I will not settle for looking at you only when no one else is about. But I will settle for making love to you, my dear young man, forever if you like. That is what I will settle for and nothing less will do.

There was a blessing on my room that day, and on the sudden doorbell of that day that made me stop and drop things for the little nervousness that I somehow could not pull away from.

Boy-o, we sit on the floor of my Chelsea room and I am confounded by your youngness when you say you love me, for I believe the coming avenue of days and slopes of night can only promise us imperfect summers and the winter's pinch. But say it again, say it and we are changed, we are our own discovery and my breath stops, darling and darling and darling amen. Yes and amen.

During the autumn term I took you home to meet my mother, the rhythm of the stopping train checking and explaining to mark our approach to Grately Station where Mr Heath from the garage met us with his car. Sitting in the back with you, I saw him look at us through the mirror. It was not an appraising look, but I took your hand and felt it tremble and wished us back in Wellington Square, books and bedclothes on the floor, our immortality contracted, and I love you. Think me beautiful and I'll be persuaded of the world's majesty.

As we went up the drive, Mr Heath said: 'I think your mother's out. Passed the car on the Andover road about nine ack-emma. Didn't see me though, or I'd have reminded her it was this weekend you were coming.'

I said: 'I expect she knows, and anyway she never locks the door, so we'll be all right.'

It looked as though my mother had forgotten our advent, but it was never easy to be sure. The house was empty except for a favoured chicken called Crossed Beak, because it had a crossed beak and had to be fed by hand, and only by my mother. In the kitchen the Esse was out and surmounted by a large common cat. You looked surprised and pale and I knew I could not live without you. A shower of dead and upturned flies covered the windowsills in the spare room where you were to sleep, and I swept them into the wastepaper basket. I didn't remind you that my mother had never recovered from my father's death because you knew and understood. I was in my own room, not far from you although an empty room lay between us, guarding our impulses with bared teeth. My mother's Geiger counter, I thought, as we went downstairs.

The house had a wan, perished look, as though it were up for auction, perhaps because the boys weren't at home, perhaps because it needed the cosseting it was built for. The dogs hurtled about barking in the downstairs loo and I let them out. You were very nice to them, and I could see they appreciated it.

There was a paper bag of eggs on the hall chest and I made scrambled eggs for us while you laid the table and looked at the paintings in the dining room.

You said: 'How soon can we go back tomorrow?' and my heart split and I said: 'Three-thirty train from

Salisbury, and let nothing stop our lives.' 'You're a wonder,' you said. 'I can't stop looking at you.'

We walked down the drive and into the village after our eggs, the big houses on the left and the cottages, the pub and the church on the right. Down a short drive, foursquare and white stood the Rectory with which Jane Austen's absolute assurance would have been perfectly agreeable. Frail sunlight dredged the forms in the post office window, the knitting wool, fish slices, hair-slides, butter dishes and string. I introduced you and we bought Mars bars and ate them. You said, 'Darling', and I knew my soul's restitution could not be until we were back in Chelsea and unable to breathe for wanting.

The car was outside the house when we got back and as you shook hands with my mother, she said: 'Do you think I could borrow a cigarette from you?' You said, 'Of course', and took out a packet, and about seven cigarettes fell on to the gravel, which was a bit damp. My mother said she was dreadfully sorry and that we could arrange them on a footstool in front of the study fire and they would soon dry – and had the kittens been born yet? Since I had not heard the threadlike lament that usually attended a successful accouchement, we hastened indoors and I opened the cupboard under the stairs and looked in. 'Nothing,' I said. 'She looks as though she could do with a bit of encouragement, I'd say.'

My mother said: 'Tell her she's a good brave clever girl and that I'll come and see her in a minute. I think we'll have scrambled eggs for dinner.'

'We scrambled the only eggs for lunch,' I said.

You looked so young. My mother had not expected it and she was somewhat *bouleversée* by the seven years between us, although I had told her I was older than you.

For the rest of the weekend I tried not to look at you. I did not want my thoughts seen by other people.

Now it is different. My battlements are foundered. I am stripped and must parade the desperation that once I put away, to attend another time. Yet you will always be my disturbance until I walk into that bright extraordinary sea.

I had been married for about ten years when I read it in the papers. You'd killed yourself, and I thought, my boy-o's dead, and I went on looking at it, and felt as though I were somehow suspended in a bit of silence, and thought, no, and thought, my boy-o that I loved is dead.

I sat on the sofa, and thought of the first time in Cheyne Walk and the last time, and the lovely in-between times, and all my murdered happiness and blithe unfaithfulness. And I felt the pain hold me and keep me, worse than the pumping pain of childbirth, yet something of that to it, perhaps because of your youngness. I let it tear away, and with the pull, I felt inside a little blood because I knew I mustn't cry, so simply put my hand over my face as I had done when we had packed up. I could not engage with the ultimate assassin, and did not cry and spilled my coffee. And thought, how dared you die.

I thought all of it, but locked it away, as I always had. I thought, bring back the too-quick Sundays and the rainy embankment days when we went to bed until some kind of tomorrow took us.

You are too close to my centre, my amputation, Genesis and twin. Sometimes I wondered who might make you wonder what I was up to after we left the Academy, the now-and-then dawdle from bed to expert bed. Don't hear it from someone else, but not from me either. Nor find out details or complications, nor why I am pale and panicky. I watched you to see if you were watching me.

I looked at the newspaper again because I had to think of you once more. Because after that I would lock you up forever. Or cry forever. There must be none of you for me or me for you. I have the little photograph of Ellen Terry that you gave me, and one of you and me. That's enough remembering. And if small other things wriggle into my remembering, I'll manage.

That little rill of cold air that skimmed over me one day, and you lying across me, a light day, a bright day and the window open and just a ribbon of cold air suddenly. I said, 'I'm freezing, put something over me, there's a good dog.' Something thumped a bit inside me, and I said, 'I'm going to be thirty next birthday.'

You said, 'Thirty's nothing,' and I loved you my best of dogs. But I felt cold. Cold.

I said, 'I'll go home and get a few things, and see if I've got any mail.'

I looked at you, asleep, and thought of the noises you make when we make love, and how the sounds of love and pain are the same. And I dressed and walked down Oakley Street, with the little rain damping my hair, buying cigarettes on the way back and I thought, will I ever be as happy again? Never. I know it.

But the cold feeling took me again, and when I paid for the cigarettes, my hand shook, and I thought, Hob the Devil is abroad, and ran back, and you were in the bath. I said, 'I met the Devil and he said I must leave at once. Oh, get out darling, let's do it again.'

At the Festival of Britain, my stomach is shaken and seems to uncouple. I think, if I love you, everything will be all right, and feel the shake again.

I spread my hand on the heavy small table to show us both the just-bought ring again, a cabochon garnet like a drop of mulberry juice. We are charmed by ourselves and by the ring and we sit facing each other drinking coffee at the iron table. The chairs do not support us comfortably, their legs tripping and rocking, and pigeons crowd us, petitioning, pecking too near the hem of my New Look frock.

I think, if I love you, then nothing can happen to us. But I know that it can and say nothing, since forged honesty is my passionate apprentice and I need your happiness.

What money we have will manage us a cigarette each and the fare back to Chelsea.

We are doubles, sometimes locked away, our thoughts removed and incomplete and sometimes most desperately, most wonderfully locked inside each other's guard, stupid with the afternoon's long love, hair damp and lips and lashes, stirring our infinite loving fusion.

Curtains haze the window in blue poplin, and the world is gone in silence, too soon taken, our promises blown.

I think, perhaps everything will be all right.

We never talked about anything important, boy-o. It was the necessary silliness of the post-war years that made our lives so lovely and so destroyed them. You waylaid my thoughts, and were the speck at the corner of my eye. Even when Hob the Devil was astride me, I thought Oh soon, oh quickly, oh darling.

But reading that paragraph such years later, I thought

only, rawly, of that first real job, that took me from you and Chelsea.

For Coventry and my first job I left you, and will see you on a Sunday. I am not yet a tramp but I'm afraid it looks as though I shall be. It's your fault for not being here.

Coventry is a great devoured city, a stretched-out warrior lately wounded, still armed, with tough, compassionate houses and thick meals of tinned peas and tea. I love it. And, since it is three-weekly, I am afraid there is plenty of time for me to betray you. But Sunday quickly come towards me, bring you to me, me to you. But do not trust me.

I read of your death again and think, you were eighteen and I was twenty-five at the beginning – lightweight stuff. Now I'm forty-two and saw you a month or two ago, and feel I may die myself.

I felt I had heard the sounds of war long before they reached me, but had not yet seen the war through. We had never talked about anything important, and now could not. And I thought back to our beginnings, all of them. I thought of Coventry and of how it bothered with me, securing me and loving me. And how good and interesting the work was. And how I was, of course, hellbent on other beds than mine, but I think you didn't know my perfidy.

I spilt my coffee, and spilt my coffee again and the complicated agony took a run at me. I thought, and thought, I'll be there by the midnight train on Sunday morning, I'll come down on Sunday, I've bought a perfectly wonderful new frock, black velvet, you wait. I said it, I thought it, I wrote it, and didn't say what else I was doing, only thought, don't ask me, don't wonder, don't watch me, but don't altogether trust me. I love you. Love me.

And I knew I must stop the keen run of remembering, but only thought how I never told the boy-o of the night of the doorway in Coventry all those years away. I lay in bed and in the dark across the road, a door, a gold rectangle in the black, quickly opened and three or four women came out, silent and with dark headscarves. And after them four men bearing a coffin came, careful and touching, and walked along the road. There was a beauty and a candour about it, and I never told you. Now it's too late for telling, for any telling, and I have only time to think, the boy-o's dead, and a stop inside me, a blunt cry like an animal's, and my life contained in it. And I thought, I must get on with things, I can manage, I have managed before, everybody manages.

Boy-o, I remember loving you with such immediacy that we could hardly waste time taking our clothes off, oh please, oh no, oh yes, oh quickly, and I thought of the going-awayness of looking at you. Make a fuss of me, go on.

I did not weather it.

Walking on the Embankment in the afterwards of love. Settled thoughts and borrowed opinions I will never have to make me forget any of it that was so lovely – silly that my whole life foundered on the floor in Chelsea and fell away from me. That joyful first purler, that bruised my life.

But we never talked of the wrongness about us, that was our rightness too, and a kind of perfection but for our lack of talking. And one night you pulled me open and burst the sometime bubble we often felt between us that stopped the moment caught. I knew we were finished, and that it was not my perfidy. I put both my hands over my face, and did not move, and could not speak, and knew I would not survive.

Boy-o, I felt I would not move again, and knew a depth of agony I would never lose and sometimes slowly coming out of sleep I felt only the measured bleakness of another day, my stomach inside out, my life full-stopped and underlined.

And I couldn't cry, except suddenly when you boiled me an egg to eat before the taxi came. Then I could. It was the egg you see, the egg just sitting there, and a piece of bread and butter. I sat there with it in front of me at the end of the table and cried, with no sound. I didn't eat it. You kissed me goodbye. Your asthma was fussing you.

I worked quite a bit, and wept every day, pushing from me every thought and memory. But it cuffed me back and I emphasised my desperate life with the occasional fix of sleeping with someone. I moved away and did not go back to Chelsea where I was afraid of seeing you, or both our ghosts. I wasn't quite all right, Jack, and sleeping around was an anodyne so weak that I thought, let be, and shake my sensibilities, because that's all I can stand. And I wept.

Did I write to you and say, 'It looks as though I'm getting married?' And if I did, what did you answer? I wasn't quite all right, Jack, but they were all very nice and I felt sure I would be accepted, for I was silly enough to believe that having my name in Debrett's and Burke's would act as some sort of talisman. I was hardly all right, Jack-in-a-box, and I knew I would fall, twisting and turning through people's minds forever, passing little thoughts and tunes and memories as I went. I will not pass you, boy-o, not quite, for we have shares in each other's immortality.

I am a Daughter of the Regiment and I kept my father's letters in an envelope, but I tore up yours and threw them in the fire because I was going to get married and it seemed only right. Before they burned, I read upon one of them: 'Darling . . . I . . .', but because I am a Daughter of the Regiment I had to do it. I had to.

I say, really? When are you getting married? Oh, soon. We shall have garden furniture, and Liberty curtains like everyone else.

Really? Gosh.

Yes, really and gosh. Into the whale's maw in my wedding gear. There are roses at the hotel, and this afternoon at the reception I will forget my overdraft.

I was fine. You didn't come. Well. Perhaps you were with someone else.

Boy-o, that afternoon when we watched the bounce and rattle of rain and ate toast in bed. Nothing prepared me for you, for this, for the absolute despair that ripped me from my ordinary self.

But I was fine, and stayed fine, and when I visited you much later in a mental home after your mother rang me, I was still fine, and took a chocolate cake I'd made, and a scarf I knew you'd love and I was as fine as anything. You said, 'You look absolutely divine, I could eat you,' just as you always used to.

We were both fine, of course. But something inside me split and pulled away, and I thought, come back. It was a small feeling, but it stopped me looking at you.

I was a bit tired when I got home. That was all.

After I was married, you asked me to lunch in your new flat. I was forty-two by then, so you were thirty-five, I suppose. I said how pretty the oval white plates were.

We are nothing to do with each other now, but we

are not strangers either. You do not look at me when you say, 'Giving you up was the only really unselfish thing I've ever done', and the words still ambush me from the dark side of my memory, beggaring my silly life. But now I must change step, for we are two grown-up people having lunch, and I look away from our other lives and out of the window and I know that I will weep for us both without let for all my life.

That year I sat on the sofa and gagged over my coffee. And I thought, the boy is dead, and remembered Chelsea, and the patches of sunlight on the carpet.

You'd better put your fists up next time round, small fry, I fight dirty these days, and I'll punch you where you destroyed me, you shit.

If only we had talked, instead of buying rings and playing conjurors and music hall and looking at each other as though we were a concentration of each other's concentration.

I thought of my little treachery and how I loved you with a kind of anger, while I enjoyed it. And I shut away everything although you sometimes leaned against my thoughts.

I became quite bright, but was still embattled, and for the next five years I did not think of you. Once I thought, you had a fine cutting edge. I liked that. As though something hounded my memory for a second. But I turned away from it, only aware that there was perhaps something strange with me, though no more strange than a petticoat showing. And I took care that I was far too busy to think of anything but the tasks in hand, and knew it was necessary to become the best, the very best at everything I touched. This I quickly became, and since I was already a matchless cook, transforming the house was nothing. In a little time, I went through it like the Flying Scot. Frightful fireplaces were torn out, the walls flayed of wallpaper, and I sat in the kitchen tirelessly making loose covers and curtains. I did not sit down ever. When I heard the children fighting, I hit them, and a good thing too, or so my friends used to say. Everybody thought I was marvellous, and I began to think they were right. The place was squeaky clean. Ashtrays timidly essayed by guests were removed and emptied before the click of the lighter was heard, and I realised I was indeed marvellous, and moreover approved on Speech Days. One of my oldest friends once said, 'But why does it all have to be so perfect?' and with pique, I said, 'Because I like it like that.'

I thought I was all right, but I felt strange, did not sleep well, and was often afraid, as though something were going to happen. I had a feeling of unreality that had been familiar to me in my childhood, but then was made better. And I felt myself unable to belong anywhere, that I had only one dimension that soon would go. And once, half in sleep, I said the boy-o's name, and woke.

One winter afternoon in 1968, I went upstairs and lay on my bed and began to cry with such force that I thought I might never stop, and went on crying for a long time and with a thin pain inside me that I couldn't identify, but that had a keen comfort to it that I was glad of. After about three-quarters of an hour, however, the doctor was sent for because it was assumed that such crying must portend something wrong with me, and blubbered with unbecoming tears, I stumbled down to see him in the drawing room. Dr Q. was a nice man who did not know me well, since I was very seldom ill, and at that time I still had considerable confidence in the medical profession. He questioned me kindly, murmured something about a menopausal breakdown and depression, prescribed tablets, and suggested a visit from his colleague, a psychiatrist.

This colleague, Dr Y., a nice shabby exhausted man, came a few days later, also questioning me and making several erroneous assumptions I did not correct. However, in view of his tart rejoinders in twelve years' time, it is worth noting that he then considered me hypersensitive and markedly altruistic.

The suggestion that I should spend a few days in a mental hospital I did not feel was inviting or necessary, despite his additional statement that mental hospitals were much improved and even quite nice these days. And he smiled reassuringly.

I believed him, since he seemed a nice man, but settled for out-patient shock treatment, and tranquillisers. And since I was, as he described me, seriously disturbed, I accepted both, though not without a rattle of nerves in my stomach, which, as it happened, would last for the ensuing eighteen years at least.

I rang the friend with whom I had arranged to go to the theatre, and told her I had now become a mental patient, that I was both disturbed and tranquillised, that if this was what the change of life was like, I didn't want to know. I said that what I desperately needed was a bit of real crying, but no one would let me, and I wept a little into the telephone, rather hating the way I suddenly couldn't manage, and wondering why, and I said I couldn't come, unless I stopped being a mental patient in the next hour. She said she was very sorry, but she wasn't altogether surprised, and had I perhaps never got over the boy? I said, 'I don't know what you're talking about. Have a nice time,' and put the receiver down.

When I had my electroconvulsive therapy, we took the puppy so that he could destroy the hospital grounds while I was in the hospital. The staff were charming, and the shock treatment could have been a great deal nastier, and produced, first of all, a predictable but short-lived amnesia and a somewhat misleading state of euphoria. And for me, something else. As the euphoria cleared, small, further pockets of recall invaded the stock I had already, some of which were unfamiliar, as though they were not mine, but belonged perhaps to times before mine. I didn't take it seriously, since I had had a few strange experiences in my childhood which had not proved particularly significant, but put them by, bought loose-leaf paper and pens, and wrote for about three hours every day for days, giving the results to our beloved ex-au pair girl, Laila, to type, which she did, neither questioning nor commenting. I was, she now says, extremely shaky, and very unwilling to let her come into the house. I felt a good deal better, but the puppy felt rather worse, since he was largely unwalked and lay curled and watching me reproachfully, his blanket chewed to shreds.

The stockpile of memory grew, kept in order by the mental docketing that I had always used, and the recall needed only an occasional aide-mémoire to open some box or other – a sound, perhaps, or a colour, or a piece of music, or best of all a texture. And all these had been discovered when I was a child truanting my thoughts away from the bang and flitter of flies on the hot schoolroom window and finding a useful freedom from it.

So I was better, they said, probably because they

believed in tranquillisers and not in writing, the cradle that always rocked me. And they said on no account would a good cry or proper talking with friends *ever* do. Shock treatment, sleeping pills and tranquillisers, they said, would be just the thing.

Electroconvulsive therapy, at best a somewhat hazardous treatment, did not, of course, produce more than a superficial effect on my unhappiness, the cause of which I had buried so deeply that even I myself could not identify it. It had, however, unexpectedly provided me with a sharper perception of what my hive of recall contained. As to the drugs and their adverse effects, they merely masked my symptoms. Such drugs were not so sophisticated when I was nursing, and their prime use was then in calming the patient in order to encourage communication, and not as an end in themselves.

Nonetheless, to an extent I seemed better both to myself and to others. That is to say that whenever I saw Dr Y. I answered, though listlessly, that yes, I was rendered insensible each night by Mandrax, and that I was eating reasonably well. The enquiry as to whether I was still turning things over in my mind always perplexed me, since that, I assumed, was the function of a mind. However, in order not to disappoint him, I returned an evasive reply.

The world turned a little, and I was forty-seven and standing in the kitchen with a gut full of tranquillisers in 1969. And I said, 'I am forty-seven,' as I had said, 'I'll be thirty next birthday,' to the boy-o and felt that cold rill of air on my shoulder in the flat. I was fine though, now, and slammed and latched my mind and locked it.

Something happened. Something happened as I stood there that quite emptied me of all other bits and pieces, and could not be described, nor comfortably believed. I was alone then, and it was quite an ordinary day, and dim, and what happened was not exactly outside myself, yet not altogether inside my perception either. It was an immediate experience, with a difference to it, so that words could not be happily used.

It seemed to happen within my senses, as though they had opened out, and peeled back to take an explosion of consciousness that I felt, and saw and heard. There were plangent colours and music, all of light and fire that poured into me a perilous knowledge and goodness, and a joy and beauty intense enough to give me a hope almost fulfilled.

It was as though I had pulled back a curtain from the beginnings of the world and my own life was stretching and contracting to take the newness and the flowering in me. I felt strong and light, as though I might fly, and as tired and drained as if I had flown over deserts and seas. A consuming happiness filled me.

If this was a heralding, then I will keep its truth and substance in my journeying thoughts forever.

It is not possible to say how long this experience lasted, or if it would have been apparent to an onlooker. It may have been of the duration and appearance of a *petit mal*, but since I was alone I could not tell, and it was years before I was able to investigate this or the experience that followed. I could not move immediately, and felt exhausted, although there was in me a great happiness.

I went upstairs and lay down, and played carols on my tape recorder. I felt quickened, and drew and wrote, as though my life had perhaps knit together a little, and I went down to see my children, and saw that upon the forehead each had a black circle. I was frightened and kissed them, and felt it must mean the Black Death, and that I expected it.

When I went up to my room again, it was changed. Where my side of the bed had been, there was a narrow palliasse covered with rough, brown material, canvas perhaps, and I lay down upon it, but with difficulty, for I seemed ill. There was very little light over that side of the room, but I could see something on the other side, perhaps a rush light or tallow dip, but most of the room was dark.

I was in terrible pain, and dying, but I do not know what it was with me. I had swellings and a fever, and I was restless. All the time I could hear the regular knocking of wood on wood, as though something were being built outside that had to do with my dying. I was not a woman any more, but a boy of about twenty, and deathly ill. I was wearing some sort of long shirt, perhaps dark green, bulky, and round my head I felt there was something golden, I do not know what, but I felt a kind of charge run through me. There was a young man sitting at the end of the bed looking at me, and that is how you sat last time, but I don't know if it was you. You look different and I am dying. Am I at last that boy you always wanted me to be? Then take me with you. Take me. The charge inside me lit and darkened.

But I don't know if it was you, and though I sometimes think of you sitting there, just as you did before you died, my life desperately and horribly changed from that moment, and I felt only fear, and the trail of corruption for the next eighteen years.

The ambulance came for me in the early evening, and took me to the hospital, and since Dr Y. had told me that mental hospitals were perfectly acceptable now-adays, I felt as settled as was possible in the circumstances.

Upon arrival, it did not appear unpleasant, and I did not, at that moment, feel in the least apprehensive. Although I had only been in hospital twice in my life, I had after all done five years' nursing, and could see no reason for disquiet.

Certainly I felt a sudden sprinkle of nerves when I went into the day room, but I dismissed it as natural. The general impression of grubbiness was less easy to accept, but I assumed it was my imagination.

The female patients' day room was on the second floor, and led into their dormitory. I sat there. 'Go and sit next to the duchess,' I was told, and I sat next to a woman who was obsessively embroidering.

There was something disturbing in the atmosphere, and an anxiety that eventually generated itself to me, and I was not too deeply drugged to feel a sharp physical fear, and to be aware of the smell that accompanied it – dirty lavatories and corruption under a wrapper of solace.

For some reason, I felt then and later that it was important that I should never show fear, whatever happened. All I knew was that there was something bad about this place, and for that reason alone, I began to shake, and wonder if I might ever get out, and wonder that this place was called a hospital.

I was violent. They said I was violent and that was why they knocked me about. Two male nurses knocked me about, knocked me about, I fell on the floor, I couldn't speak or breathe or struggle, just fell on the floor, fell down and lay there. They were quite big men, I was frightened, I fell down, some sound coming from me, I blacked out, my cheek against the floor, the green carpet, I blacked out.

At the Enquiry they said that I was violent, they had to knock me about. They said there were no witnesses. They said that at the Enquiry. I was forty-seven and my life began to black out when I heard this.

They can say anything.

From that first incident a tumult of nerves was set up in my stomach which could not be quelled. Wickedness is often sensed before it is encountered, even when it is shielded by a *louche* respectability.

I don't know how I got into the cell or when I was thrown there, but I felt as though I were coming out of an anaesthetic, and my belly crept and swam as I got to my feet. I was wearing a white gown, wet and cold, and was taut with fear. It seemed to me that I could die in this place. My head cleared a little, but I felt stiff and strange. The wall in front of me was covered in obscene and explicit graffiti, usual in public lavatories but hardly to be found in hospitals, and a bubble of sick burned in my throat, and weakly threaded down the front of my gown.

Stupidly, I believed that I could simply open the door, walk out and tell the world about this place, and I tried.

The door was irrevocably locked, no one answered my shouting and I began to shake with a terror I had never felt before, and which has followed me in nightmares ever since. I tried to force my hand through a hole near the keyhole, as I would do throughout the night, each time pulling it back stitched with splinters. Three weeks later the splinters were still there.

In the cell was a bed, and a tiny window high up which I tried to crawl up to. Sometimes an eye looked at me through the peephole, but no one answered or in any way communicated with me, and, my guts liquid with fear, I screamed all night, knowing that now I might never escape and that no one would come. I screamed until I could not scream any more, and then lay on the bed and prayed every prayer I had ever known from the nursery onwards. I thought of my grandparents and Chichester Cathedral, and fell into a thin sleep. I felt that for the first time I was with wicked people, and wondered what else they might do to me, and perhaps to others.

I woke suddenly an hour or two later with the need to pee, and shouted, banged on the door and the wall, too frightened to feel anything, and empty of all but a desperate panic, like a dog in a thunderstorm. No one came and I wet the bed. I slept again, cold and with shallow nightmares, waking every few minutes in the same maw, the central light still blazing down on me. I wanted to die, longed for it, wished it quickly done. I did not feel I could go on pretending to be brave, and did not know that the fear of this hospital would drag after me for over eighteen years after I had left.

I apologised for wetting the bed when the night sister let me out next morning. She seemed the only human being on the staff and was shocked at my blood-spotted hand.

And I ran down the corridor in my white gown, and away down that corridor again in all my waiting night-mares, thinly screaming for help, humanity, for God, and for my safe childhood and a sworn advocate's hand to drag on and know best for me. For my changing life, so reasonable for many other women, had slipped from that reason into the clamminess of dread.

Round the room sit the patients, looking ahead, not speaking, sometimes smoking, and I with them with empty desperation, because I know I have to take care what I say and behave myself. Weighing up the time lopped away between injection and injection, tablet and tablet is impossible, and I know only that I surface from each drug till the next in that web of apprehension that is now part of me. Meals I sometimes remember, and once I said the Winchester Grace, Benedictus Benedicat, as a prayer.

I am lying on my bed in the dormitory. Light comes through a fanlight over the door to the day room where the night sister sits knitting.

I am a mental patient and I lie where I am put, on the top of my bed in the dormitory, my mind half rubbed out by drugs. No one will ever believe me again and I want my mother. My stomach is rancid and my senses sprawl, but some of us are asleep, us mental patients. The stupor keeps only a handhold on me, but suddenly when I see him I shake it free, and am shocked sane but no, no I see him at once – the kind male nurse – no Mummy, no Mummy, say no no no.

He put his hand between my legs, pushing and fumbling into my cunt, said, 'Is this what you want? Is it?', took my hand and made me hold his cock, no no, take away my memory that is dirtied take it, take it, my life unfastens me.

Lovers do such things with love and joy, wonderfully weeping for the little death to crown their divine agony.

But now I can never, will never – cannot love again, nor will I ever feel safe. Inside me is the shout, and outside me is the bleak whimper of an animal, pulled

124

from me, and take me home, take me, take me. The shadow slips away to his covert, but my skin creeps still, and I am marked as prey, since I am gentry, a captive, and have wet myself with fear. And I know that nothing need ever be heard of me, nothing revealed.

They said there were no witnesses. At the Enquiry they said there were no witnesses.

I did not run away that night, but later – later – after – running, running, running, through the grounds, a great arc of red leaves on the grass, and ran and ran but didn't know where, and fast, as fast as I used to be when I was a sprinter, running for a safe place that would hold me safely and gently, where no wickedness could get me. But the dream of footsteps behind me stopped my breath back into my throat, and they found me and, terribly, brought me back and thought it amusing.

But the night of the dormitory I could not move, and lay awake half the night staring into the pale dark, and when my husband visited me, once more I did not say anything, just asked if I could go home, and when they would not allow it, could only make that whine again that animals make. And we sat, and the other patients sat and sat. I felt sorry for them, but my own sick fear numbed me too much to feel more than anxiety for their duck and glance. We were all impaled by silence.

I was in the hospital for three weeks and in a continual state of fear, particularly when I had to take off my clothes for an X-ray. I was frightened of being alone with the man who gave me an intelligence test, and although a brush with what was probably an electro-encephalograph seemed innocuous, I trusted no one throughout my sojourn.

Most of the time I sat silently in the room, like the other patients. Sometimes I went down to the men's day room, since they were pleasanter and seemed to like me.

I was standing in the female patients' day room when I heard the voices. There were only two of them, and they came from about eight feet away from me and about ten feet above the floor. One of them said, 'You are going to have to be braver than you have ever been before,' and the other said, 'You're going to have to do it yourself.'

They were quite objective, and I accepted them, although it was the only time I had ever heard voices, nor did I hear them again. It has taken eighteen years for fulfilment.

Florence Nightingale, of course, heard voices four times, wisely remaining mum and merely recording the information in one of her little notes. Fulfilled in due time.

For the ensuing weeks of my captivity, my conduct was impeccable, because I was too frightened to behave in any other way, and because I felt I must be discharged if I were to survive. I took my pills, talked to the other patients, even smiled at the staff and eventually discharged myself with the help of a young male patient who filled in the form for me.

And I went home. I was dirty. My trousers and jersey were the ones I was wearing when I had arrived at the hospital, and now they smelt of fear, of sweat, of sick, and of pee. The ugliness and terror of that time would darken my senses for years, and tablets procure my silence.

At home I described what had been done to me, but quickly, with revulsion, the sides of my mouth sticking together. My own house seemed alien, and loneliness still sliced into me, sending me to the lavatory with the taste of bile in my throat, as it had for the last week of my captivity. I remembered the cigarette butts swimming in shit in the hospital and retched and thought of how I had sat on those rank lavatories with shit pouring out of me and felt that no one would save me. I felt I had no being, for shock wipes your brain clean, and since I did not know I was in shock, there was no one else to recognise it, and soon I felt as unprotected as I had at the hospital. I knew how my condition should be treated, but could not do for myself what I had done for the soldiers I had nursed, and the clammy horror plastered itself to my mind.

I could not recover from the remembered fright that short-changed my life. I would not see friends, and would rather cross the road than encounter a man. I lost interest in everything, and was too afraid to answer the front door until we had had a peephole put in it. I no longer liked or trusted doctors, and in my consciousness forever swung a constant re-enactment of the hospital. Nothing quickened me, and love was no longer beautiful, but ugly and frightening.

Since psychiatry seemed the only treatment for my state, a barricade of complicity met me the moment I left the hospital, and I was forbidden to talk of the ordeal and immediately silenced with drugs. My inner scream for help echoed back at me as it had done in the cell, and after a while, I knew I was being held incommunicado. My instincts and principles, once healthy and defined as apples, were peeled and I could trust no one.

I cut my wrists. I cut them because I was a coward and I cut them because I was thoughtless. I looked sharp and bought the razor blades the day before, and I looked sharp and made certain the house would be empty. I felt lonely and guilty but I was not at all afraid, and I had two baths, one for getting clean and one for getting dead, and washed my hair and put on quite a lot of scent.

I thought, into whose hands do I commend my spirit, for God's sake? Who will love me? Who will be there? and the thread of scarlet sprang against my wrists and aridly stopped, and I began to weep for the struggle and the failure. I thought, you failed, and you've buggered up people who love you, and I got out of the pink bath water but still struggled and sawed, and meanly bled.

I sat on the safa and wept and lit a cigarette and picked up the telephone and said, 'I'm sorry – I've – I'm sorry—' and great, bloody tears banged down on my dressing gown, and I wiped them away with the heel of my hand like I did over the egg you boiled me, boy-o. But I didn't think of you. You were dead.

Ambulance drivers are impatient with failed suicides, they give you little shoves and say, 'Come along, dear.'

I commended my spirit into the hands of a short, clean, manicured psychiatrist who would not allow me to speak, did not wish me to say I still felt dirty from that place because that was nonsense, and you shouldn't attempt suicide for such a ridiculous reason. I tried to explain the other reasons that were attached to it, but he didn't like that because I might have betrayed a sensibility and a knowledge that he would not care for. And he flipped his notebook with a sound like a whipcrack.

After three weeks of reading magazines in his mental hospital, I looked at myself in the glass and thought, for God's sake get up and fight. School's not out yet.

But I couldn't. The drugs checkered my thinking and lost me my balance. To try and expunge the effect of my ill treatment, we moved house four times. And each time I carried its fear with me, and the outcome of the Enquiry was predictable – there were no witnesses. The classic physical signs of shock had long ago become apparent in me – loss of body hair and cessation of menstruation. Subsequent appointments with Dr Y. elicited trumpery enquiries about mood and appetite, and the insistence on more drugs with the attendant side-effects of vertigo, incontinence and blurred vision. Any reference to the nightmare that still hung over me was treated with studied disregard. I was still having bad dreams, and was still afraid of every corner I turned. The people who should have been easing my distress were keeping my mouth shut with sophism and chicanery. Unsurprisingly, breakdown followed breakdown.

My mother, appalled by what she had heard, asked me to stay in Wiltshire and since I was the only girl, and also since she had nursed me through so many illnesses, she may, perhaps, have felt she knew me better than her other children. Certainly she knew the amount of strain I could take. I went, gladly, but still with a feeling of remoteness, as though I belonged nowhere and was separated from other people by some concealed web, light but inexorable. I needed the familiar trespassing of old addictions to calm my disposition.

The house had the superficial appearance of most medium-sized country houses with a few acres of land and a drive choked with weeds, but with this one a certain delicacy had to be exercised with the occupants if visitors were to be tolerated. For example, one must gain entry to the house without tripping over the chickens in the hall. And it was useful to remember that a sick calf might be lying in the kitchen on the dog's blanket, that seven cats slept in the study and did not care to be disturbed. And that the heaving mass of dogs in the nursery might very well belong to someone else, and had probably been in the house for weeks without my mother having noticed.

Inside and outside my mother's bedroom in Wiltshire were humid piles of dog baskets, dog treats, old dog collars, dogs and occasional kittens, while in her wardrobe still hung memories of her life as a Bright Young Thing. She seldom threw anything away, considering that if you kept your clothes for long enough, fashion would begin creeping round again. For her life and fashion stopped in 1940 when my father died.

After his death, and with scant knowledge of almost any animals, she returned one day from Salisbury Market with a Jersey calf in the back of the car, from whose loins sprang eventually a herd of pedigree Jerseys of some worth. These were generally to be seen embedded udder-deep in mire outside their shed and were accompanied by a crowd of disreputable cats who surfaced only for provender placed on the pre-war lino in the kitchen and frequently refused. Constantly preceding resentful visitors up the drive was a scatter of confused hens, whose perfunctory efforts sometimes produced a pale egg of meagre proportions. My mother cared for them devotedly. Unfortunately the first lot of hens were killed by my brother's dog. My mother was very brave but said: 'They were all personal friends of mine,' and the next lot were housed in the hall, a hazard for unwary callers.

The dogs, two rough-haired dachshunds, for the most part neglected, spent their time putting up pheasants, stalking the hens and barking at the cats before sinking

130

exhausted on to the drawing-room sofa until the next meal.

The house and garden gradually became an animal sanctuary, but my mother did not encourage us to apologise to our friends for its state. She would have considered it vulgar to do so.

In middle age, with application and with love for her charges, she earned their trust, learning to milk cows, to deliver calves and if practical, nursed any ill animal in the house. I once went into the old nursery to find a calf lying asleep on a dog blanket. She said: 'Not very well, poor little thing. I shan't get the vet, it does more harm than good because it frightens them.' If any of her animals needed the vet, my mother stood by, stroking, murmuring and comforting, taking away fear and pain, however mucky the job proved to be.

She did not intend to have all these animals, she simply acquired them. A stray cat had only to appear at a window and she would throw both door and window open, crying: 'My poor darling, come in at once, you can't sit out there in this weather – come in.' And the dazed cat, padding inside the house, would find the kitchen table groaning with unsuitable food – digestive biscuits, chocolate peppermint creams and perhaps even a saucer of brandy to restore the poor traveller. It was no surprise that my mother was beloved by these cats who multiplied so adorably and so carelessly.

She didn't care much for small children, preferring them to develop a little more before overtures were invited. Once babyhood had paid out its gauge and spanned the strapping gaucherie of boy and girl, then my mother was at home to them. Requests for something to make holes in conkers with did not floor her. She answered at once: 'You need a bradawl. There are two in the bottom of the fridge in the larder. Take only one. And I imagine you will need string. You will find some in my bedroom by my bed marking the place in my book. Make a note of the page you take it from.'

My mother's vagaries were distinctive and she was in a sense celebrated for them while my father was maddened and enchanted by everything she did and said.

She had, for instance, a propensity for withdrawing from her own parties and once, overcome by boredom, hastened up to bed where she was later found enveloped in Turkish cigarette smoke and doing the crossword.

A situation of greater piquancy must have obtained when a guest at one of my parents' dinner parties, having noticed his hostess's absence from the table and happening to glance through the window, spotted her in the garden planting lettuces by torchlight. It is true that she was a gardener of talent and imagination, acknowledging experience while eschewing conventions, and thus was her frailty spared.

I never met anyone quite like her. She was a clever, beautiful and unsettling companion. She wrote, sometimes almost illegibly but with immense style, and her letters were sometimes written on blotting and occasionally on lavatory paper. All that mattered to her was that she could write on it. She abhorred pretentiousness of any kind and was cursed and cherished by everyone who knew her, because she did not consider any job to be beneath her.

When she was a child, my grandfather gave her an uncommon animal called a coati, which was brought from South America. Thus, with god-like charity, the *Shorter Oxford Dictionary* states: *An American plantigrade carnivorous mammal of the genus Nasua (family ursidae), resembling the racoon and with a remarkably elongated and flexible snout.*

That may be, but this little visitor, perhaps the quarry of a waggish boot-boy and certainly a stranger to plumbing, might yet have enslaved the MP's young daughter who was to become such an intriguing and formidable woman.

My mother kept a photograph of her coati and a few years after my father's death she found it when she was turning out her bureau, and showed it to me – a furry animal, not unlike a fox, I thought at the time, and a cheerful fox too. 'My coati,' she said, pronouncing it 'quatty'. 'So sweet. I loved him. And I miss him, you see.'

As I struggled through the pungent turmoil in the house, I felt the warmth of alliance that might be relaxing and perhaps fruitful. Not this time, though, which was to be more difficult than any visit had ever been. We sat in the study, unable to talk on any level. I felt sick at the idea of talking about the hospital, and my mother, who knew what had been done to me, found it beyond her imagination that such things should happen to anyone, let alone to her daughter, and was incapable of saying anything. Yet both of us knew that talk was healing, particularly since I had been silenced from the day I came out of the hospital.

We sat and smoked, and tyrannised the cats.

My mother said: 'Write something. Get something down on paper. Well and cogently written; it could do some good – perhaps help a lot of people.' 'Think of the law,' I said. 'Anyway, I will *never* want to put it in writing – it would all come back, particularly the smell.'

I looked out of the French windows. The garden was like a staunched sea-bed. I smiled upon its neglect and murmured: 'I really rather love it like that,' and my mother said: 'Oh, I so agree. Absolutely. The dreadfulness of perfection. I used to love it of course, and even now, one feels, well, as though it should be a bit tidier.'

I said, 'Balls,' and she said she didn't really think I should use that sort of language, and when she was my age, she didn't know, well hardly, that such things existed. And she said: 'Those two curious experiences you had before you went into hospital, tell me more about them – not the voices – voices are not unusual at all.'

I described them, and she said: 'That first one sounds like the Illumination. Did you feel it was some kind of religious ecstasy?' I said I couldn't possibly tell, and she said one seldom could, that perhaps I was merely one of the Illuminati, nothing unusual about that, and that the second experience might have been some kind of reincarnation, a phenomenon which she had always found difficult to believe in.

We went up to my room, and after a little while she said: 'One way and another, the propensity you have for these sorts of experiences may mean that you have qualities which certain kinds of people need to destroy. You get the same thing with animals.'

She swept some dead flies off the windowsill, and sang a little of 'Goodbye Dolly Gray'. It was wonderfully sustaining and emotional, her voice not quite what it had been, but even then only a bit diluted.

When I left, she suggested I find a good reference library, spend the day there, and check everything I could, the Law, psychology, not psychiatry, and religion to start with. I said I would, and took home with me a basket of rhubarb, a jam jar of cream, and a Spode coffee cup that I promised to have mended for her. And the offer of a very, very naughty kitten for the

134

children. I said we already had two very, very naughty kittens from the last lot, and they weren't kittens any more, and the puppy didn't like them or the tortoise, and would she like the goldfish we usually brought back from the fair because they seemed to turn arse-side up and die every time, before we'd even got them home.

She looked anguished as I left, but didn't suggest I try and forget all about the whole thing, nor did she tell me not to worry about it. Instead she had given me something to sharpen my teeth upon, and I felt understood and strengthened by one who had known me from birth, loved me, and whose principles and beliefs were under the same command. And I thought of the elephant table in Eccleston Square and my grandfather's injunction to 'flush 'em out'.

But the psychiatrist's consulting room soon put me in my place, and once more I began to feel despair and loathing at injunctions to keep silent about my aching distress. I knew other people were being force-fed in this way, and I thought of my grandfather's advice to 'flush 'em out' if chicanery were suspected. It was suspected, to say the least, but the 'close ranks' policy was also in action.

I went to every reference library I could find, and settled down with notebooks and pencils.

Photocopying the sections of the Mental Health Act relevant to sexual assault with wilful neglect by hospital employees was swift and simple, as were the relevant parts of 'The Law Relating to Medical Practice'. In another part of the library a version of the fourth-century Hippocratic Oath I found interesting and made a copy. And I discovered a transcript of Blaise Pascal's Mystic Amulette, that described his Illumination in 1654, an experience which seemed comparable with my own.

For me the most important books in that section were about thirteen volumes of Professor Jung's works and one by one I lugged seven home and applied myself to them. I read as much as I could understand and understood as much as I needed to become aware of a mind as remarkable as a ring of bells under water.

I wanted to be explained to myself, to ask questions and be given answers. Lately I had seen six visions, and described each on a minute piece of paper and filled a note pad with numbers, letters, geometric figures, a human pentagram, a Pythagorean triangle and details of the Great Pyramid of Cheops. It was as though I were sometimes inhabited by another personality, as though another mind and personality had taken me over.

The visions were more complicated. I had described them minutely on paper and in some cases had drawn them, and again I had no memory of having done this. I felt that it was best not to tell anyone about any of these curious happenings, so I kept all my notes and drawings secret.

One of the most interesting visions was a great black clock face that almost filled the room. The hands and numerals were of gold and both hands pointed to noon. The I saw two children, twins perhaps and neither boys nor girls, one mounted upon a huge shire horse, the other holding a sword, and once I saw in front of me a thick sand-coloured wall with the words 'Mittere me O mittere' inscribed on it, and almost immediately I heard a voice say, 'The Will to Splendour'. I knew 'mittere' was the Latin for 'send' but could go no further and had no idea what the voice had meant.

The next vision was not complicated, but it had a strangeness. I saw a bleached and rocky sea-scape. It seemed very hot and I felt that it might be Spain. There were two boys, again twins perhaps and aged about sixteen. They wore identical black knee breeches and white shirts and both were sitting in a small open boat with between them a coffin. I did not feel this coffin was empty. I was a part of this particular vision and was standing on a rock watching. The date might have been about 1660. I saw this scene several times.

The last vision was that of a lamb or other small white animal being led up the centre aisle of a cathedral. I felt happy when I saw this.

Every now and then I felt as though I were on the edge of something unexplained and took my typewriter into the sitting room where I slept on the floor, using the excuse of writing a script for one of my friends. With abrupt simplicity, the dog would fall asleep in the dining room while I played empty tapes on my tape recorder into the early hours.

Sometimes I heard a might-be buzz of may-be voices on the tape, but often I fell asleep, or stopped and wrote poetry for my niece and nephews, and wrote my own epitaph, but thought it only moderate. I thought of the Illumination, and felt myself a starveling for lack of information, and did not know where to go for answers, although the essence of its pull I found I could recapture quite easily in the middling darkness. But did not know if it were indeed the Illumination, or some passing dream.

Once I turned on the television and watched again the Miracle of Elche, so richly, sweatily, gloriously, Spanishly wailing and devout, the gilded Virgin a rouged boy, gold-dusted, his hands uncurled in a benison. And once, peeling from my mind like a child's transfer, the burning, hanging fruit-colours of my parents' India in the thirties, brightly, jealously imagined as a child. I felt a quickening from these sensations, for until then all forms of creativity had been sliced from me during those three weeks at the hospital and all love and fine memory taken. My life had become a looking without seeing, a touching without feeling, and an uncurling of apprehension, footsteps at my back all the time.

My life gaped like a cadaver during the years after the hospital and my values were scraped thin by drugs that changed my personality. There was nothing in my mind or appearance to suggest that I had ever lived. Indeed, it was as though my early life was gone from under me, taken by the night caller who knocked at my uncertainties and sucked my essence dry. A threshold seemed to mark my differences from other people, and small, silly shocks could unfasten me. I could answer the ring of a telephone, but if the call was one that I must make and knew might summon a human answer, then the receiver spewed panic in my ear, as though by dialling I might call down again the headlong-creeping thief who, threatening my mind's establishment, would see the giving-way of all my gathered strength.

I cannot go out in the dark, my nursery fears being realised, I cannot. And if I must – if there is no help for it, then I am grazed with apprehension for hours before, and – double peril – must ring for a cab.

I cannot see the charitable ambulance without a liquid gallows-drop of fear, and even now, waking in my own bed, I hear the lock's grim vacillation and the key's supremacy, a harsh and bloody union that held me in the cell. In my head I hear my screaming and in those later Shanghaied years wake thirsty for more sleep to stun my memory forever, and with my eyes still closed I say no, no, no . . .

I see the single light that was never turned off and the high, small window beyond my reach. I remember the obscenities on the wall and feel the splinters in my hand. The strutting voice still consumes my mind: 'Is this what you want?'

If you are a mental patient, you will be given absolution but no remission, and your eccentricities will be impounded and judged whether you are the rule or the exception.

Yet, sleeping on the floor of the sitting room, with Sam compactly coiled in his basket, I felt an occasional clarity touch me, and touch some element or trace in me that I still kept.

I rang my mother, feeling my voice discompose the room round me. She sounded exhausted and absented, but this had been noticed since my father died. I said: 'I think we're going to have to move again. I have read all that stuff, and taken in a good deal, but the nightmare is gathering itself to pursue me again.' I wanted to say it was like being crapped on, but somehow I couldn't.

There was quite a long pause. She coughed and asked what I had done with the right-sided Staffordshire dog I took last time – one of a pair, she said, so pretty and with a basket of flowers in its mouth. She was fretful, santery.

'You mean the Spode cup,' I said.

'How could you mistake a cup for a dog?' she said sharply.

'For a what?' I said instantly reminded of Carroll Dodgson's brilliant non sequiturs. I said I would bring both cup and dog, but I knew from her sudden oldness that it might not be necessary.

I had really rung her to say there was to be an Exposition of the Holy Shroud of Turin, and that I was going there to ask a hoped-for miracle to purge me.

But I did not. There was a vagueness clouding her more than usual, and I decided to talk to my aunt about it instead. There was to be a pilgrimage, and ingenuously I felt a spike of hope that by this miracle I could pull away from the threadbare principles of shuffling tallymen who deadened my convictions with shoddy. They knew that I still screamed in the night from the screw that had turned in me, and the corruption that secured it.

You can do a whole lot worse than to believe in miracles. You can do worse than pray. And there's nothing wrong with faith. If you're up against a pretty nasty set of circumstances here on earth, then it's worth asking help at a higher level. Having a lot of relations in the Church didn't mean I was different from anyone else, it meant that belief was quite important, and one was encouraged to remember it was there and could be used.

Since my experiences about ten years before, I had believed in nothing, hadn't prayed, hadn't even been to church. I felt the Church had trampled on me, so I trampled on it, and even forgot my own religious teaching, simple, robust and loving, and with the added blessing of humour. I felt a terrible despair, as though I had done something wicked. But had only loved someone too much. And that had been behind my portcullis for years.

I had only heard of the Holy Shroud of Turin when I was a child, from my grandparents, and accepted everything they said about it without quizzing them. But when, in my fifties, I began to read Ian Wilson's scholarly and fascinating book *The Turin Shroud*, I found I was without any knowledge of it at all.

I was quickened by the descriptions of recent extensive tests, and by the volumes of evidence pointing to the Shroud's authenticity which I found tremendously exciting and stimulating.

But, retching, I discovered crucifixion to be one of the most vicious and considered forms of brutality employed in execution at that time, and very far from the euphemistic representations we have learned to accept without scrutiny.

These descriptions and illustrations left me wrung out with shock and humility. To seek a miracle in such a way, through such a death, whether authentic or not, seemed terrible and obscene. But not to put from me such paltry squeamishness seemed to show in me something small and wanting, and the writing, so matter-of-fact and uncoloured, pulled me together, and reading the first chapters, my belief in the Shroud's genuineness grew and thereby my hopeful miracle. Proof, at best a dry descended word, seemed to me foreign, and the trumpery tag of fraudulence had pierced it now and then, through each shift of time since the fourteenth century.

An impressive denunciation is that of Pierre D'Arcis, Bishop of Troyes to the Avignon Pope Clement VII in 1389, which begins thus:

'The case, Holy Father, stands thus. Some time since, in this diocese of Troyes, the dean of a certain collegiate church, to wit, that of Lirey, falsely and deceitfully being consumed with the passion of avarice, and not from any motive of devotion, but only of gain, procured for his Church a certain cloth, cunningly painted, upon which, by a clever sleight of hand was depicted the two-fold image of one man, that is to say, the back and the front, he falsely declaring and pretending that this was the actual shroud in which our saviour, Jesus Christ was enfolded in the tomb, and upon which the whole likeness of the saviour had remained impressed, together with the wounds which he bore.'

This 'certain cloth' I had to see. But I felt a nervousness catch at me each time I thought of it.

The familiar and dreadful trappings of pomposity and sanctimony were utterly eschewed by the clergymen of my family, and their divine simplicity I had always taken, shaken and accepted with love and certainty. I had not been brought up to doubt truth, and I knew that good and evil existed, and would need to be noticed occasionally. Certainly one's instincts would prick up their ears at the first eddies of real iniquity, and I met it at every psychiatrist's appointment. But there was nothing to be done. Gagged by the cosy guilt of others, I would be pushed further into the impotence of break-downs until I was ultimately shut away.

It was no use displaying values and tenets that had been wounded – that was not what they were for. You were embarrassing at dinner parties and first nights, and caused uneasy dislike in the psychiatric profession. Certainly I had done a little more desultory work, in the shape of watching relevant documentaries, with a note-book, and had also read part of the Rampton Report of an enquiry, in the reference library. And I took out a book on mathematics. These things seemed necessary, so I simply took notes and hid them in case, sometime, they showed some usefulness.

But the tug of me, the pull at me, was the feeling that, before I made the pilgrimage to Turin, I needed particular counsel, and from someone who had known and loved me from birth and whose faith was still intact. I took a bus to see my aunt.

As I rang the bell, memory paced me to the childhood scent of tobacco flowers, and my grandfather's gentle, humorous sermons at Chichester. She was his daughter, and praise be, my proxy mother, and knew of the disjection of my life, abhorring it as one's flesh and blood might feel each the same wound. The nine-year thraldom of silence that destroyed me, almost destroyed her as well. But I was sustained and lent sinew by her love.

In the library, she said: 'Sit, my darling, and tell me what it is.'

I told her where I was going, not needing to say why, for to her, miracles were a part of life, whether sought or not. For her, as for me, words, human beings and bread and butter, all were marvels, and she charged me with hope and enthusiasm for this most needed pilgrimage.

Since my conscience had felt a little pocked since my arrival, I eased it by lighting a cigarette and asking if my somewhat dubious goings-on as a young woman could jeopardise my chance of a miracle.

It's true there was a slight pause before she answered.

I mustn't, she said, be such a juggins. 'Listen,' she said. 'If He was going to worry about that sort of thing, He would hardly be in His present position, would He? You've been submitted to a very unpleasant form of corruption for ten years, and that's exactly the kind of thing He likes to get His teeth into. You're just as worthwhile as anyone else – why shouldn't you have a miracle too? Don't expect anything, do a bit of believing and some praying and don't fuss. You'll probably enjoy it.'

I said I felt panicky about the whole thing. 'Don't be. No one's going to refuse you help in Turin. God's not one of those ghastly psychiatrists, just someone special who thinks you are someone special. There are lots of miracles going on all the time – I've had a few, but sometimes one has to wait for a door to open, and it can take time.'

I said I couldn't remember how to pray. She called me a goose, said it didn't matter, something usually goes up, whether one was conscious of it or not.

'Goose to you too,' I said. 'I wish you were coming with me.'

She said: 'God forbid, what a dreadful thought. It'll be like Lourdes, I expect, plastic Madonnas and rosaries. Don't, please, bring me awful souvenirs, however holy, just yourself and all details.'

As we walked to the gate, I said: 'I wonder if I will ever dare to tell anyone about those two voices I heard in 1969.'

She said: 'Well, I shouldn't ever tell any of those psychiatrists, or you'll be behind bars again before you can say "knife". They only believe in pills – slot machine minds, you see. Disappear the cat and leave the grin to fool people.'

She kissed me. 'Goodbye, enjoy it, don't forget I love you, and don't expect magic. These things take quite a bit of strong faith. Don't get sunstroke.'

The febrile late summer spread exhausted over Kew Green as I walked on it, and a few children's voices popped here and there, carried off by the evening. I went home, and whether I was trying for a miracle or simply seeking knowledge I was not sure, but I felt I must absorb all I could about the Holy Shroud, before I joined the Turin pilgrimage.

The Shroud is a fourteen foot strip of pale linen, smudged with the sepia indications of a human body, without art, and uncontrived. It is this linen that Pierre D'Arcis described urgently as 'a certain cloth, cunningly painted', and that has caused clouds of controversy for hundreds of years.

However, Secundo Pia, a lawyer, photographed the Holy Shroud in 1898, thus becoming witness to the most remarkable revelation. He took two exposures on the night of May 28th, 1898 and it was nearly midnight when he got back to his darkroom. As he developed the plates, there appeared upon the negative the two distinct images, frontal and dorsal, of a man laid out in death, sombre, uncompromising and of a formidable beauty, barely hinted at in the Shroud itself. That the man in the Shroud was a crucifixion victim is almost certain – it was quite a common form of execution at that time, and certain indications on the cloth might be taken as proof of this. But that it was indeed the Saviour's image that revealed itself to Pia still awaits ultimate confirmation as far as this is possible, although the weight of evidence cannot be dismissed.

In the next few days, I set forth to discover all I could about the pilgrimage. The travel agency, whilst readily admitting the existence of Turin, knew nothing of any pilgrimage, and somewhat blanched at the word 'Shroud'. Ergo, I sought information elsewhere, and with it hurried back to the agency, who, greatly relieved to hear it was merely something to do with religion, set to work with zeal.

Within a few days I had the information I needed, money changed hands and we smiled upon one another.

Behind the counter at the jewellers, the Signora turned upon me eyes as lucent as fidelity, and her hands moved carefully amongst a tray of silver bracelets like a catch of fish. She smiled and wished that she might go with me. I promised to bring a memento back for her, and she asked hesitantly that it be blessed for her. Yes, I said, and yes again. She smiled and said she was glad I was wearing the little black cross, and wished me Godspeed.

It rained, and suddenly. And rained, fizzed, spun, bounced, buzzed, zipped, cracked, spat, whipped and chattered. I waited, opened my mouth to speak, and so did the Signora, as I waited again, waved, ran.

We would be in Turin for one day, and for that the joinery of writing went into my flight bag, and the tumbril rattle of pills to process my mind and flatten my judgement. In the corner of my thinking I saw the ring we bought, boy-o, but it was only the thin, dull blood of my wrists. I didn't mean it. Only for a second, a second, a second. You could have waited, I thought and slammed my mind shut. I made some Lapsang, checked my passport and emptied my mind.

At the station next day, we stood anxiously, strangers to one another and to the whole affair, each of us a scrap, a grain, a suspicion, a drop, colours and shapes changing and moving like amoebae, as elated and stricken as holiday-makers. Patting our passports and glancing over our shoulders for some mysterious assurance, we encouraged small comforting smiles to pass quickly between us, as who might say: 'I am a comparatively seasoned traveller, I can instruct you as to the whereabouts of the lavatories, and no doubt if and when there may be tea, and perhaps sticky buns, even.'

There may have been those who essayed the lingo, murmuring, 'Ecco', perhaps, or, 'Si', and swiftly turning to the window, for fear that someone, unnoticed before, might suddenly strike up with them some dreadful foreign conversation, someone whose name was known to be Brown, yet now disgracefully proclaimed himself 'Bruno'.

But in truth, there cannot have been many conversant with a pilgrimage to Turin for the Exposition of the Holy Shroud, and we settled like quiet well-mannered children. Opposite me sat Iain Davies, a priest, whose company I would enoy for most of the journey, and with whom I fell to talking almost immediately. The disclosure of my wartime nursing record prompted him to call me Florence, tending, as time and acquaintance-ship grew, to Flo, which lasted and to which I answered throughout the visit.

The atmosphere was unstrained and pleasant. The two charming older ladies in our compartment, abashed by Iain's clerical appearance, spoke in low consecrated voices, fearful of offending the cloth. Their pastel Crimplene generated a deal of static electicity, and at bedtime a modest firework display was ours. Until then, a pleasing lassitude laved our spirits, and curiosity about each other was tempered with the delicacy demanded by our slight acquaintance. Thus did we smile, doze and eat, and like clean, good children, thus were we cared for.

But as the land of Nod beckoned, our mild manners of a sudden became as the fury of the caged beast. For it was discovered that throughout the train, our seats sullenly refused to discharge their duty, would not

147

become the bunks expected, remaining loathsomely resilient and buttressed, despite our maddened efforts. Stripped of control, of *bonhomie*, and even of manners, voices rose, matrons and elderly gentlemen, hitherto courteous and well-tempered, shrieked help or compensation.

Once or twice, some man, perhaps anxious for a plaudit or two, would roar that since the mechanism was perfectly simple he would deal with it, and would take, as it were, a pitiless run at the problem, achieving torn ligaments, strained muscles and a considerable loss of dignity.

Even the women, though of a milder disposition, sighed and glanced at their watches, and clicked their bags open and shut, noting with despair the neatly folded polyester nightdress, trimmed with satin bows, all awaiting the sandman's caress – if indeed sleep existed still. For tempers were high, headaches prevalent, perhaps even feelings of disillusionment began to arise, most shocking of all thoughts, and most heartily to be forgiven. As soon deprive a lion of his Christian as a pilgrim of his sleep. And the long hot Turin day lying ahead of us like a shaft of gold.

Iain and I, slightly hysterical, escaped along the corridor to find and give out blankets. Exhaustion caused hilarity and we spent a good deal of time leaning against each other giggling and smoking.

But soon we were too tired to laugh, and dragged ourselves along the train, handing blankets into each compartment, where things were beginning to right themselves at last. Eventually the shouts of battle faded, seats became bunks, and Iain left us for the night – for the proprieties must be observed, even on a pilgrimage – and we would meet next morning.

The barbs and thrusts of shared disaster reaped felicity for most of us next day, one smiling upon the other, a blissful amnesty, each pardon begged, the blame embraced and cherished with the day. It was a scratch, no more, for we were in Turin, and the sun of Italy emptied on to us like a cut melon as we stumbled from the train.

Security for the Shroud was tight, and the *carabinieri* buoyantly discharged their duties, pretty as pictures, bright as a bullet. A public unisex loo, of noble architecture, lent majesty to a simple function – even in Italy I had not looked upon its like before, but to screech to a halt in the doorway yelling, 'Oh my God!' as one of us did, displayed a kind of prudish vulgarity. After all, comradeship relaxes and unity is strength.

Great swatches of children ran and bounded hopla, stridulant and smudged, and through them I threaded and bought a medallion for the Signora. For myself, a little table, ice cream, mineral water. I felt myself wince for Malta, but I was grown up and in Turin. Malta, hanging on to the petticoats of my childhood, did not need me. A thin, small boy shambled towards me, immensely showing off, wanting tributes and ice cream, no doubt. I offered, he refused and drew slowly in the spilt ice cream. Thick hair palisaded his forehead and fell over his eyes. He licked his fingers and said, 'I am Carlo, who are you?' and I said, 'I am Benedicta Lucia.' He nodded and did not smile and ran away, his impecunious shoulders labouring beneath the holiday shirt, taken by his mother from the line, the pleached vine above it bunched with small uncertain grapes.

My heart felt a little soft and I took out my notebook, but put it away and finished my ice cream. People stood outside the Cathedral, blessed by the sun, and I joined them, excited and nervous. I don't know how I felt, but I think it may have been like love, so badly did I need to see this Shroud, sometimes forgetting why, sometimes remembering, putting it from me, yet taking it to me, like the long drink of someone or something you love and must have. I stumbled from the outside light and foolery and under the dark wing of the Cathedral, quickly crossing myself like an extra. First, the absolute darkness and the gradually moving crowd, and then I could see it.

It is small, and far away and lit, and I feel uncompleted. My need is forgotten, and instead there is a crying in me for the cloth, for its undefendedness, a child newborn and early dead, the cord not cut, the rebel's shout blockaded, the boundaries of life killing time, the takers taken. I see my beginning as small, as fearful as the end that is so tender and separate from the far crying of me.

It was so quickly over that I did not think or feel or know anything. Though I thought something pulled at me, engaging my memory, and for a second the pitch of my life altered. But I thought it of no consequence. I walked away and felt the pull again and still it did not seem of any consequence, and I thought: 'Well, I have seen the Holy Shroud, and felt only a little crying, a little jumping inside, no more, and certainly forgot to pray, so I expect that is that.'

I went outside into the spread-out, flat heat and the clutter of tadpole children that skittered and yawped and knocked against each other. I felt in me still the changing pitch of childhood, and thought that something turned and lifted. But there was nothing, simply the hidden fear that I had felt for years. For a second I thought, how will I end, then? Coiled in that same fear?

But I thought it for a moment only, and became relaxed again and charmed by all the pleasant strangeness of this place.

An inkblot of priests standing in a square ticked my memory and I ran up to them with the Signora's medallion for blessing. A quick murmur over it, and they moved off for lunch like a tram. And so did we.

After we had had lunch, three of us went into a cool, small church. Here and there knelt the prudent shapes of nuns, like punctuation, their whispering nicking the air about us. Beside them, great shopping bags spilled lemons and bread upon the dusty floor.

Lassitude had knocked some of the experience from under us as the day thinned and lengthened and words spun away into the still air without answers. It grew dark, and the Exposition was over for that day. Children played weak suppertime games in a playground, and left, bumping into one another from tiredness and twilight. My notebook was virgin, my feet killing me. A low, hot restaurant gave us cheerful dinner, but I fell asleep between each course, extinguished by the thought of those lawless bunks.

In the city, the Cathedral stood dark and perfect, like a drawn sword, and far away at the end of it a Mass was going on. We stood just inside the door and watched the tiny brilliant figures, scarlet and white and gold, their voices guessed at, like toy actors propped in a cardboard proscenium.

Standing near us were exhausted ardent nuns, their weak eyes damp with piety, their spectacles misted with hope and guilt.

The moment we crept out of the Cathedral, we were

almost immediately lost. And to be lost in a strange town, after dark, where nobody speaks your language, and worse still where you have an assignation with bunks, is an experience no one would ever wish to repeat. Back and forth we trod, across squares, through dark alleys and down narrow steps. Sometimes we were pulled up and anchored by shop windows full of satin cushions and reproduction French carriage clocks, or lulled by the warm light of a restaurant still open, its jaunty late laughter trickling over the pavement. We hailed anyone approaching.

'*Stazione, per favore?*' elicited a flux of incomprehensibility, while the less extravagant 'Where is the Railway Station? We wish a train at midnight,' called forth merely a puzzled silence, until praise God, the glorious advent of the police. Straight from heaven, they listened, grave, dignified and self-aware. They nodded, and with immense, heroic gestures pointed away and into the heavens from which they had descended, and where we knew our train must await us. Thankful and blessed, we bowed our heads, and like a chevron of small animals, rushed forth, murmuring and twittering, and found and flung ourselves into our train, now so deeply loved that nothing could tear us from it. Without a word of calumny we embraced our cheerless bunks, for soon we would embrace our own beds, the unexampled memory of this day behind us and within us.

In the years that came after the pilgrimage, I was sometimes besieged by thoughts of that murdered Son whose image hung in hot Turin's cathedral. It was a cherished secret, lagged close and removed from other secrets that now gave room to this one honourable thought. Though I still dreamed dark dreams, strangely I felt that something warmed me and gave me small summertime words, as though someone said: 'It's all right. Nothing bad will ever happen to you again. I will see to it,' and in a sprawl of uncounted nearby thoughts, this one lay inside me like an infant lily.

Yet while I was in Turin I had half forgotten the reason I was there. The pallor of heat and exhaustion having smudged my sensibility, I lacked thought, and thus the need to pray seemed a lesser and a gentler need. I had become different since I left the hospital, changed and changed again, my life as unredeemable as a pauper's wary debt. And yet in the still air of Turin I had forgotten to ask a miracle. Nanny would have said it was a fine thing to get there and forget the errand that had brought me; to sit beguiled by sun, ice cream and Carlo and forget the grimy laceration that had effected the journey whose long-for end might halt my battle. She would have reminded me that a miracle would wash me clean again – a nice clean girl for Mummy, she would say, or the entire pilgrimage might be held of no account and it would be early to bed and no tears.

The hidden child in me sent a clumsy apology to the God I had never known well.

And though it is true that the recent carbon dating process has shown the Turin Shroud's inception to have been during the Middle Ages, I still have a faith and a certainty that I cannot explain nor yet dismiss.

My mother died quietly and tidily in an expensive London nursing home.

While she was there, she was no trouble to anyone and did not even wear the new nightdress I had bought her, which hung over the back of the chair beside her bed. She looked small and wanting, yet was there, to be spoken to without answer, could be touched, the skin loose and thin, the bones only supposed.

I did not feel grief or loss, but despair for one I had never consciously counted an ally, yet now did, and most desperately.

And I remembered once, in Wiltshire, my five-year-old daughter dragging one of the dogs into the bathroom in my mother's house and heard her say: 'I'm going to put this so sweet dog into the basin and I'm going to wash his hair and comb his ears and give him some porridge.'

'Nix,' I said, 'you'll do no such thing. It is six o'clock in the morning and you can damn well do what I tell you for the next twenty-four hours because we are staying with Granny now.'

'Over my dead body,' my mother said from her room and I heard her switch on her electric kettle.

'Sarah,' I said, tripping over a dog-basket outside the dressing room, 'put both those dogs back in the cloaks and go to bed.'

'Nobody likes you when you say things like that,' she said. 'Dogs don't like you, horses don't like you, ducks don't like you—.'

'Go to bed,' I said, 'or I'll beat the hell out of you.'

'When are you going away?' she said, 'because mouses don't like you either.'

I gave her a light whack. My mother came out of her room carrying a cup of tea and wearing a nightdress, a duffel coat with 'Taffy Two Gun' painted on it in red across the back, and gum boots. My son, Tom, advanced towards her down the passage.

'Darling, who is this small boy?' she sighed.

'This is Tom,' I said, 'your grandson. We're staying with you.'

'God,' said my mother, taking an absent-minded bite out of a chocolate biscuit before the dog could snap it up. 'But you never told me all these children were coming – who are they? The cats will hate it.'

Tom said, 'Mummy, do they have a kittern here? Can I have a kittern to play with? Can you paint kitterns? I would like to have a green one.'

'My poor cats,' said my mother.

'Granny is tired,' I said. My mother said, 'On no account am I to be addressed as Granny – it implies age and I am not old. And couldn't one of these children go down to the pub and get a packet of De Reszke cigarettes for me?'

'Mummy,' I said, 'it is about five-thirty in the morning, the pub has never sold Turkish cigarettes, there are not lots of children, only two, and they would never be allowed in the pub anyway.'

'I would be allowed,' said Tom, 'but I don't want to go because I'm going to build a huge pile of spit down in the hall and people will be very grateful to me and I'm going to show it to Granny.'

'The cruelty of that word "Granny",' murmured my mother, 'and what frightful clothes your children wear, darling. You never wore pyjamas with ducks on them.'

'Jumble sale,' I said shortly. Tom climbed on to her bed, jumped about, fell off and cracked his head on the mantelpiece. His mouth opened and he turned a face of tearless anguish to me. I didn't give him a chance. 'Bloody go back to bed,' I yelled and my mother said, 'Poor child, he'll remember you said that, they always do.'

Without surprise I heard my daughter say: 'I don't like these dogs after all. I'm going to throw them away.'

I removed her from the bathroom, slammed the door on the dogs and hurled her into the dressing room. My mother said: 'I don't know who all these children are that you keep talking about but you don't seem to have much control over them.'

Superbly, she called to the children: 'Now then you two, come here. You may each have a chocolate biscuit, and later on you can give the cats their breakfast if they'll lower themselves to eat it. But now you are to go straight to bed and to stay there until I give you permission to get up.' They went. The bribe was worth it.

My mother turned to me and lowering her voice, said: 'Darling, listen. If you don't want lots of children, you should go to something called Family Banning, a sort of clinic I believe.'

'I did,' I said. 'I felt they didn't really believe a word I said.'

'You should have written to *The Times*.'

Her letters had been published in *The Times* since she was a girl, a success matched by her sister Barbara.

Pulling her duffel coat round her, she said: 'I think I might do a little light gardening today.'

It was snowing when I drew back the curtains, and I thought, like hell you will.

The inconstant waters that sometimes took her mind to strange back streams had settled to a quietness, and she came and stood by the window with me.

'How funny,' she said. 'I thought it was spring.'

Once or twice in the nursing home I said: 'Mummy?' and tried to examine how I felt about the long discovering of her voyage and of mine. 'Mummy?' I said. 'It's Benedicta,' and I remembered how, long before Nanny did, she got to my bedside, guardian against bad dreams, sore throats, wet beds, and noticer, though not always remarker, of tears.

Once, my daughter came with me to the nursing

home and fed her mince, and with assurance and gentleness told her how beautiful she was. And I picked up one of my mother's old Lenare photographs and said, 'Mummy – look. This is the most beautiful woman I have ever seen.' She had smiled with shameless pleasure at her memorable looks, and it made up for the mince which she spat on to her plate.

Later on, lying thinly on the bed, she fell back in time a little, and talked about my father for the first time since his death. The nurses said she had once got out of bed and taught them how to dance the Viennese Waltz.

We sat with my mother in the nursing home, the clean room bearing away our silly words. She seemed hardly there, needing only a familiar touch and voice to help her win the unknown conflict. We listened to the nurses' muted cheerfulness outside the room, and my brother and I fed her through a pipette, the liquid running from the corner of her mouth. They had asked me to do it, since I had been a nurse, but I felt a difference about this – I wanted to say: 'Yes, but this is different, this is not a patient, this is my mother who took care of my ill childhood. It is different, different.' But it was not.

As I looked round the valueless room with its sickroom warmth against the winter afternoon, I felt miserably: 'Oh for God's sake Mummy, can't you just die and then we can all—.'

'All, what?' I thought. 'Go home? Have a cigarette? Strip off the tacky guilt we feel every time we come to see you?'

I stroked her hand, and wondered if such a germ-free room was a good place to die, or whether the careless succour of dogs and children would be more loved and comforting.

Since we were all in bed, asleep, front doors locked, dogs coiled in baskets, we missed her passing bell the night she died. The telephone rang, before I was out of bed. I remembered, and for no reason, how she had always hated being a grandmother.

Our funny, maddening mother had died in the same way as many others, yet when we went to see her in the nursing home the next morning, tiny and dead though she was, there was something resourceful about her. I thought, Lombard Street to a China orange she's already arguing with someone somewhere.

My brother kissed her forehead and said: 'She still smells just the same, did you notice? A sort of Mummy-ish smell.'

We were little animals, snuffing the familiar smell of our dead.

It was white cold when we had finished thanking everyone and collecting things. I had learned not to have any feelings, since last time I cried it led to the darkest corner I had ever turned. My feelings had been managed by aliens ever since, and I must never be permitted to talk about anything. I allowed myself a cautious pang as I got into the car.

Since black humour was a speciality of my mother's, and since her funeral held the elements of a Tati film, we were assured of her enjoyment, even if our own were debatable, for it was an uncommonly bleak and long-drawn-out affair, to say the least.

Since the service took place in London, and the burial in Wiltshire, a long wintry drive was necessitated for all of us. It did not surprise us to discover that there had been a strike of undertakers, nor that it was the coldest day within living memory – if that is how you care to put it.

Thus, and characteristically, our mother was late for her own burial, by quite a few hours.

We clumped about in the village churchyard in enormous coats and boots, throwing admiring glances at the newly dug grave, trim, tempting and edged with imitation grass. The day darkened. Our ears stiffened, our blood congealed, and the air was crisply feathered by our breath. Sleet snapped at our raw faces as we exchanged politeness with the unfamiliar young parson who was kind and quiet, his great shoes comfortable beneath his cassock, and his hands winter purple.

Our spirits rose considerably when, some time later, we saw the hearse unctuously turn off the road and over the little bridge, and we greeted our mother's late entrance with the affectionate irritation granted to kin.

Driving home I felt raw with remembering, for a moment, and I knew I was not ready yet to call up any thoughts. And our house that we could see up on the hill from the car seemed, like me, to refuse sympathy or comfort or ownership. But I knew we must come back and clear out each room, and buy cigarettes and Mars bars at the post office, and that after that, I, at least, would never see it again.

I thought of middling Christmases with my father dead. I thought of my mother funny, my mother clever, my mother maddening. But wisely I emptied my mind of her for some time, and when I was ready, sifted, recalled, and did not mislay her verbal elegance and wit, allowing fond quarter for remembered wrath. My life spread away behind me as I remembered coming home on leave during the war. And I thought of how my mother never spoke of my father again after his death.

For a second, something bumped inside me, and I remembered taking the boy-o to Wiltshire for one impaled weekend, when we did not dare to look at each other. I had thought, please be sure of my love, and please have another glass of South African Sherry, and oh, let's go quickly back to London and Chelsea. Here I might as well be without you and without myself.

But in the car I thought of it for a second only, and staunched it, and lit a cigarette and locked it up. I was in my fifties. Behave yourself.

Out of the car window I saw rooks' nests tethered, scanty and incoherent, to the tops of trees, and thought, this is an ending. Now we are urban. We do not belong to the holly, nor to the ivy, nor to the village. Nor do we belong to the gypsies on the market-day bus.

And I fell asleep, heavily, and full of forgetting.

It was a brittle amber day when, like birds, we all flapped back to Wiltshire to eviscerate the house and call back ghosts. The front door hung heavy, its paint peeled to sallow thirst, and our optimism gaped away from us all in no time. The usual uncompounded reek of cats' pee still issued from the study, rendering us virtually insensible, and a lack of zest marked our early labours.

There was no water and none of the loos were working, which meant we would have nowhere to wash, drink or pee, though happily this infused us with a kind of jocularity, and becoming sportive, we bumped into each other and dropped things, as Brokers' Men do.

I put my head into the nursery. It was empty, and held only the warm smell of books and dog blankets. I felt as though I had disturbed something, as if it had drawn its breath when I went in. It was standing still,

160

waiting for one of us, as it had done even after we had grown up. We had gone on sitting in there, even then, bickering, playing poker, having tea, bullying the dogs.

I had sat in there by myself when I stayed with my mother after the hospital. It was one of the few places where I felt safe.

I stood in the middle of the room for a moment, and felt an immense sadness. There would never be any certainty again, and I would never be protected again. And I knew I would be afraid of men forever now, and must not show it. I went out of the nursery and pushed the feeling away. There was no easiness in me yet.

The French windows in the study were open, and I walked out on to the terrace, a swag of weeds snarling round my ankles. The garden was bleached and drained, a fatality, one of the fallen, the trees tourniquet'd with ropes of convolvulus.

Dejected, consumed and laid waste for decades, yet its original and Italianate form and grace were still drawn in, on that exhausted, bright day. I looked across the coppice where I had once buried a plate rather than confess a breakage. While my mother never bore grudges, loss and breakage were national disasters to her, and reason and sense of proportion went for a burton.

I wandered into the kitchen garden, abstractedly looking for the cats. When I went into the house, there were a few discarded-looking people in the hall, like free gifts that haven't turned out too well. We smiled at each other. The downstairs loo still had the smell of galoshes in it, and the Italian earthenware dish the dogs always had for water was still there.

I felt I stood in the middle of a battlefield, that only I was left alive, all strife over, and that somehow I was a survivor – the survivor of a struggle that I had had no part in. Yet I knew it was my fight, and that no one could ever help me.

I felt this only for a moment. Then I walked down the passage to the kitchen where Susan was crying a bit. It was an ending for her, although like me she was in her fifties and had a family. She had come to us in her teens as a parlour maid, and had stayed until the finish, doing all that must be done, her neat black frock and white apron replaced for years by trousers, anorak, scarf and gumboots as, without hesitation, she had joined in the push and pull of life with us, the milking, the cooking, the war, the weather. She adored and cared for my mother, eschewing reproach and offence at the ageing childish acrimony, disordered mind and sopping bed that faced her each day. It was an unimpeachable personality.

I kissed her, and said, 'Don't worry, darling,' and tried not to encourage her unhappiness too much. We had things to do and she was an easy crier. For me, it was simply a further bullet to add to the others I'd been biting on for so long. I lit us both a cigarette. She said, 'There's no water and no loos. Don't know what everyone's going to do.'

'Well,' I said. 'We'll manage. I haven't seen the cats, by the way. Where are they?'

'They're all right,' she said. 'Cats are always all right.'

'I'll have a look round for them, all the same,' I said. 'Cheer up.'

I looked into the dining room, but it was empty. The portraits had gone from every room in case of burglars, I supposed, leaving huge marks on the walls like closed eyelids.

Through the window I could see the field where an

aircraft had come down during the war. I had just arrived home on leave and was still wearing my outdoor uniform. The house was empty, and I heard a sort of thump, and across the field was a small aircraft lying on its side. My heart plunged and I picked up the first thing I could see – my surgical scissors – and ran across the terrace, and our field, and under the wire, just as a young man crawled out of the aeroplane. He said, 'I'm awfully sorry about this,' and undid his jacket and helmet. I was so thankful he wasn't the Luftwaffe that I felt quite pale, and whispered, 'Are you all right?' praying that I wouldn't have to do anything, since I had only been a nurse for a few months. He said, 'Yes, we're both all right,' and another young man appeared. The first one said he hadn't noticed I was a nurse, and would I care to look at the scratch on his thumb? I did, and that is exactly what it was – a scratch – I should have offered him an oxygen tent, of course. At that time I hadn't learned very much about men. As it was, I gave them both tea, and after some telephone calls, they went off in the local taxi and the wreck was collected some days later. I never knew their names, and they didn't know mine, but they sent me a card addressed to 'the Pretty Nurse', and I felt quite grown up.

I went into the nursery again, a fiddle of nerves following me. There was nothing I had not noticed before. Books all over the floor. I picked up *Moorland Mousie*, which had fascinated every small girl when I was a child. The brass animals from India stood in twos on the mantelpiece, and in an armchair lay the ceremonial trappings of an elephant, naive and tawdry as Christmas decorations.

I felt nervous, still. It had the quiet of a set before

curtain up. My father's riding boots stood by the door, tree-d and brilliant as chestnuts, and on a table were the *Regimental Chronicle*s in a heap, with the top volume open at his photograph and obituary. I picked it up and left the room, closing the door behind me, still feeling a frisk of panic. It was as though I left behind an unfinished life, the wrench of disconnection that was mine still wailing.

My sister-in-law dressed up in something she had found, but the alien and seductive figs of Malta took my memory through and away from her, like waxed thread.

I went up the stairs, and on the landing felt the familiar despair that had picked upon me so often. It seemed to me that we had been merely guests in this house, missing the careless observances obliged by blood. I had slept in four of the nine bedrooms and belonged in none. The house was like a stray, to whom we sometimes gave a passing pat, but without great joy. For my father, having designed and had it built, then died of wounds and broke my mother's heart – and in it we had rattled and shouted, introduced friends, given parties, whispered and wept for forty years.

The familiarity of my mother's bedroom fell easily about me, the old, flat smell barely noticeable and touched with that of remembered dogs.

In the Italian wardrobe hung clothes from lost decades, all loved and kept. I touched a frock by Maggy Rouff, moth-eaten, black and spare, worn for cocktail parties in the thirties and borrowed by me during the war.

I walked down to the pub for cigarettes, and remembered picking the sloes down the drive to make sloe gin. Spines of sunlight flaked warmly on to my shoulders. I had thought I might not mind about this day, but each discovered memory seemed meshed into another – my father's death shot with my mother's eccentricities, which became painfully the boy-o's tremulous weekend visit, and now, my mother's death, controlled and reasonable as the inscription on a gravestone.

I felt a stray, like the house itself, allowed no comfortable sadness for these and other thoughts, and filled with tablets as a guarantee.

The pub was matted and dark like an old nest, as it had always been, happily not transformed by the presence of two Johnny-come-latelys in fancy cardigans, drinking sparkling wine beneath a brash hunting print in a gilt frame. Their whispered comments at my dirty dungarees and the cobwebs in my hair were understandable. They had probably seen me coming from the house from afar, and expected me to be grander.

Otherwise, the pub was the same as it had been since we moved to Wiltshire – smoke-filled, low-ceilinged and murmurous. It was easy to trip over the uneven floor, and everyone stopped talking when you went in, resuming when you'd taken your bottle of cider and gone.

Going back, past the dried-up stream, I saw the field where we used to help haymake when we were young. In the empty wagon we bunched, holding on to each other, as Billy Grose galloped us away up the field, standing up tall with the reins, like a charioteer, brown as a kipper, hair jumping and the great horse lurching and thundering like an act of God, with us nudging and tumbling like fruit in a pan.

As I walked back I thought, no, I do not love this house. Not really. Small moments, remembered because I was happy, because there were things ahead of me, and I had not yet destroyed myself or taken away my own hope and hidden my own death.

When I got back to the house, there was someone in the hall who had known my mother, and said what we all needed was a strong drink, and drove off in his car to get it. And I stood in the hall and thought, during the war, I used to dance with your brother. Before I was a VAD. I must have been young. I felt I wanted just to go and sit somewhere with him, outside perhaps, and not talk. He came back with a tray of drinks, and ice and glasses, and put it on the hall chest, and it was wonderful. I picked a few cobwebs out of my hair and said with fourteen-year-old hesitancy, 'I think I used to go to dances with your brother. During the war, I mean – I was – we were – I was quite young. About, well, perhaps about eighteen.'

He smiled and talked, but I felt ridiculous. I thought, what on earth are you saying? Why should anyone want to know how old you were during the war, or who you danced with, or whether you danced at all?

It was as though I was held suspended in a fragment of time that I could not recognise but that was important to me. I thought of myself at eighteen, and I thought of the boy-o at eighteen, and a quick agony took me. I lit a cigarette and dropped it and picked it up remembering an evening dress and how I covered my old Shakespeare with some of it when I went to the Academy. It was a little time-jump I had become caught in, and because I sensed a clumsiness in myself, I felt defensive, as if informed against, and my part not taken. Yet he was pleasant, this man, speaking, as it were, the same language, familiar and attractive. I was restored.

From the attic I took imperfect memorabilia and some perfect, and a hired van drove me home. They've done a lot to the house, now, the new people – smartened it up a bit, which it needed. They've knocked down the wall between the pantry and the kitchen, and made a breakfast room. We always had breakfast in the dining room, with the French windows open in the summer.

In the van, that day, I sat next to the driver as we drove home. In the back the sculpture banged about a bit, and I remembered my girlhood's hopeful summer days, but did not want to. I remembered the cheval mirror in the hotel bedroom where I once stayed for a regimental dance when I was seventeen. I had taken my clothes off and stood in front of it and looked at myself for quite a long time, and thought, well, with overtones of wow, and turned a little, slowly and appreciatively round and about. And I thought, I suppose eventually someone will want to sleep with me. I hope it doesn't hurt, and I hope I don't have to wait long, or I might go off. Like fruit. I thought I was marvellous.

I wondered why I was thinking such things, and said to the driver, 'Left, here, please.'

In a few weeks the nightmares began.

I am in the dark hospital again and they will not let me free. I am on a great black horse in a tiny cell, the mane smoking my senses. I burn – my wrists bleed from the wire that binds them, and my head is shaved.

With these nightmares tagging me I went to see Dr Y., and sharpish he was, evasive, and gagged me with jejune theories.

I must, he said, stop thinking of myself, and must keep busy, and he added that it was all most unfortunate. I pointed out that this nightmare had been with me for twelve years. He was nervous, and the tilting tracks of guile unseated him. I noted this and locked the entire interview away, ready to play back in my mind in the future.

But going home, I shook, for I felt that the dark was pulling me down again.

That night, the branches of my mind shook and fluttered. The footsteps ran when I ran and stopped when I stopped, and the screaming lasted all my life.

O God, the difficult, difficult birth and the easy death – the dark treachery of my boundaries and the kick of nerves. Let me do this dying by myself that I have waited for so long. The screaming will not stop – I must find the end of the mandala and the twist of hair that strangles my words and puts me back in the cell again. They took no notice of the wickedness that darkened my change, and the life that hung beside it.

I woke often, with the breath pulled from me like a last instruction, the remembered dread dogging, cat-nipping me, outrighting me and fighting me, drug-thuggery ditching me and bitching me, Godforsaking me, half-baking me, invading my mind that was once as right as ninepence.

I wrote a good deal of poetry, but then my brain suddenly shredded, and I was removed to a classy, private mental hospital, battlemented, plate-glassed and ruthless with plastic and Dralon.

There was television in each room, to give a sense of security, but I was seized with fear. The nurse who brought me Ovaltine assured me that I could always ring my bell if it were necessary. But I didn't stop trembling, and the legacy of fear clung to me, and I knew I could not lose it, or regain my own beliefs unless someone took my hand.

As usual, reason and judgement were scrubbed clear of my mind by treatment, and I felt as much extinguished by the emollient strivings of this place as by any other institution. And since I was cogently denied help, I remained frightened and helpless. I was, I suppose, fifty-nine.

Dr X., assigned to the care of my sanity, was a lubricious pipsqueak who padded about the corridors on the balls of his feet, enjoying a deal of genuflexion from both staff and patients. His method of dealing with my fear was more direct than others had been, and certainly more ruthless.

I was not, he said, to talk about it at all; it would simply make it worse. And he added that I *must* recover, that everybody did. The Venus flytrap had begun to close, this time, however, without the lure.

I began to slough off the effect of the drugs. Boy-o, all I wanted was to cry over you a little, because I had not allowed it, you see. Just a little would have done. I got twelve years of attempted corruption – soon to be eighteen – and these people were trying to make me accept something that was wrong. I felt a tremendous anger. And something inside me said, I am too good for these buggers, and I will never have a breakdown again. What my safeguard would be, I had no idea.

Snow weighted the dark branches outside, and the setting in of evening had the same promise as it had had in Eccleston Square when I was a child in moderate finery and my mother had sung 'Goodbye Dolly Gray'.

My two brothers and my sister-in-law came to see me. I knew they had no idea what had been going on all these years, and that to them I was merely a mental patient of long standing who was not worth listening to, and certainly not worth believing. They were, understandably, relieved to go, to get into their car, to drive, eased, to their house, saying perhaps, 'Well, she seems all right.'

'Yes. And at least we've been.'

'Yes. And it seems awfully nice, the hospital.'

'Yes, doesn't it? Awfully.'

'Oh very. Except for the vinyl Chesterfields, of course. Shall I give you one for Christmas?' They would laugh at this, and in my room I played back Dr X.'s interview and Dr Y.'s acrimonious words in my mind, as bright as brass.

But my mind retched and swung at the easy inaccurate phrases, and I thought, if you're lucky, my girl, you'll be a mental patient forever, because each time you ask for help with the nightmares you still have, they will sharply cut the hope from under your feet.

I remembered Grandfather saying, 'If you suspect chicanery, flush 'em out,' and I thought, there's good. There's straight. Not like these shits that I have been battling with since 1969.

But I felt the sinew in me thinning and pulling away, as though there was nothing of my own good blood left in me. But all I could do was to toady up to the staff, do what I was told, take my pills and shift my brain a little without appearing to.

I knew that if I could not extricate myself from this loathsome spike that impaled me, then I must make of myself a neat end, a comfortable finish to a silly life, more accomplished, and accomplishing more than I had done the first time, when I cursed and could not find the vein.

Thus was I softly, quietly biddable, but round each expert enquiry's corner, I felt the muscle pull me taut.

Like a rope walker standing upon a platform, I listened to expense-account sophistry, and heard Dr X.

say, 'You must recover. Everyone does.' But would not let me say how the scream curled inside me, curled and spat for over the last twelve years, carrying in its poison madness after madness.

In a week or two I would be well enough to leave. I would be Mummy's clever girl, Mummy's nice clean girl. Who, then, is a good girl? Why I am. I am the crazed mother, the mad sister, and I hear the voice of the hangman.

I am a good girl, am I not? Do I not take my pills, talk to the dogs in the Occupational Therapy room, and watch a patient making fairy cakes? Why yes, I do. I do, I do, O God.

And, of course, I never mention the sharp clamour of fear when I dream of those fingers, oh Mummy, oh Mummy, oh Mummy.

So pleasant for him, only a slightly ticklish business to put his fingers up my cunt, because no one believes a mental patient, and so easy for him to creep into the dormitory, since he was a male nurse, and just enough light to do any pleasant little wrong in sight.

I sit on a Dralon-covered armchair, and the resilience of Dr X. cancels my replies on impact.

'Is your mood stable?' he asks me. The moods of all my used-up life stream away behind me as I face him and the plastic flowers. I do not say, 'I will staple you,' but I will. I will stable you and staple you to a mirrored hell, and set you flying, and let go, let go, let go, let go a my life that you have torn from me.

You may scream as I have screamed, and bleed as I have fallen pale, and I will not hear you as you would not hear me. Bleed then, Mister, to death. I'll watch.

When I'm discharged, I thought, and return only for my moods to be checked, I will call back the knowledge

I have had tucked away since I was seven. And I will top it up with what I have discovered since, by stealth and purpose.

I asked if I might visit a hypnotherapist and talk it out and out and away from me, even if my lips bleed a little as they are pulled one from one. And Dr X., vile as an upstart with acquired power, took an expansive breath, and said I might, but wagged a finger, saying it might not work, and that certainly I must go more than once, and be prepared for disappointment. And if I heard a lift in his voice on the word 'disappointment', I dismissed it as his golf-club accent, there to impress underlings, and fulsomely I thanked him for his handsomeness.

I went into my room to savour the pleasure of tomorrow, when I could leave. In the little bathroom I felt again the oily throb of the P & O Liner that used to take us all to Malta when I was young, and the high sills so easily tripped over. I remembered the Lascar who brought me a glass of stout each evening to make me a stronger child. I found it bitter and was allowed crisps to make it go down more happily. Into my chair I was lifted by the Lascar, his nails like needles and a smile wonderfully, intensely white, a benison upon my meagreness.

I brushed my hair in the looking glass, and knew I must never be in thrall to such people again, and threw empty punches, as I had done when I was a child. But I knew it was too late, that there was now a difference in me, a shift in my spirit that would stay. I felt some big crying jump into my throat that I wouldn't accept, which I didn't want, didn't want, I didn't want it, and I thought, boy-o I couldn't manage after all. They've done something to me and I can't change it. Why did you say that to me before you died?

I brushed my hair in the looking glass, and suddenly noticed an equine toss of my head, some bravado to it, and thought, perhaps, after all, you are a horse – a looking-glass horse. Weakly I made some notes in my head – with every word at my command, and without one fluff or dry, I shall discountenance Dr X., and I spat a great gob on the looking glass. But then leaned against the door and put my face away and wept for all the gone-away days you left me with.

I went home, snapped at by the winter air, and in the car thought, am I fifty-nine, or more? Everything gone in the nightmare under the carpet.

I feel strange, as I always do after every breakdown. My legs don't work, I feel my appearance is odd, and I have no appetite. I have a friend staying and generally cook some great wonderful Elizabeth David dish, but now I sit by the fire and do nothing. I think I look like a tortoise. I say: 'Do I look like a tortoise?' She says: 'A bit. I think it's the collar.'

The months began to fall into place, and I became a little braver, catching up with the normal rhythm of life. But it was as though my faculties had no use, and I could never be myself again as I had been. I felt my early clarity veiled, and myself locked in uncertainties as simple as other people's daylight. I tried to pull into myself at least some pleasures of the senses, and drew a little, and read a little, and thought with relief of dying but said nothing.

I realise now that such feelings must be expected and acknowledged as a feature of the illness's aftermath, and that the brutal jocularity of familiars is hardly likely to improve matters.

And, tremulously, I went one day to Burlington House, to the Summer Exhibition where once my

173

portrait had hung. 'Benedicta Leigh', it had said in the catalogue. I remember looking at it at the private view, and meeting my old diction teacher. Why, she asked, had I been painted looking like that? That old red shirt – and that short hair? Actresses should never be painted like that – what was I thinking of? Although, of course, she said, she knew it was me, there was only one Benedicta Leigh. I remembered saying that it wasn't commissioned and that was how the painter had wanted me.

Even then, before anything had happened to me, I looked like a puppet pulled from the sea, not left for dead, yet hardly worth saving. But able to fight still.

My life becomes a little fuller as I decide I must never be goaded into more breakdowns, that I will simply record everything and play it back whenever it is appropriate. I behave perfectly, for I am Mummy's good girl.

I am well enough to go to a party – expensive dips handed by classy young women. On the way to the loo are the Lelys that used to be at home. The room is fat, hot and crowded. I have claustrophobia, a legacy from you, boy-o. Twitters and squeaks from in-laws who think it is a sign of insanity.

'I am sorry. I must go home. I think, quickly.' And I do, before I faint.

A twenty-first birthday party with a moon and a marquee, and I sit next to a very young man with sticking-out ears, who talks to me with noticeable sweetness. I wonder who you are and what your name is.

I appeared to enjoy these junketings, yet I feel beneath my skin the fear of 1969 curling and turning in me, something steeply hidden that I may not talk of, because

I am a mental patient with, in my throat, the sticky playground secret always remembered, the dragged knickers in the thick four o'clock light.

This is what they had made me feel, people like Dr X. and Dr Y. at their teak-veneer desks. From them I ran when the sky was pulling and tangling in the coming dark. They were the followers, the footsteps after me, the hands up me that I could not forget. They did it.

I was accustomed to these feelings, which gathered inside me as I crossed the expanse of secretaries to be questioned by Dr X. Otherwise I felt as though I had been punished for someone else's bitter crime, the cicatrice still burning in my skin as proof of my disgrace.

Bear the scar of insanity and you may as well display a broken wing or paw – your stronger fellows will be sure to injure you further, ultimately destroying you, themselves perhaps feeling some inner strain tear their vitals. Be certain none will help. You are already carrion.

And so it seemed with siblings and sometimes coincided with, perhaps, the death of a relation, making one ally less. But it existed. One wrote that he was too busy to see me, and disregarded my reference to my obvious distress. The other displayed the carking jealousy of the nursery that now sped sourly from the page.

I put my hands over my face but felt strength. Boy-o, come back. I will get a gun, get a gun, get a gun, a gun to shoot them with. It is them, they have scarred me, I will make a darkness that will fill their lives forever.

Boy-o, I am ashamed, These people need fear, they need my fear, the footstep that I heard behind me, that I may not talk of in case something gets out, and they would rather I kept my fear good and strong and close.

Dr X. will say: 'No, I'm afraid I can't let you talk about how you feel, but do tell me how you are sleeping and what your appetite is like. You are looking very well. Would you like a glass of water?'

I would like a human being. I would like my parents, but they are dead. I would like someone honest because I am accustomed to it. It is raining. It used to rain on the Embankment and we went to bed, because what else can you do?

For God's sake. For God's sake. That last thing, why did you say it? I didn't see you again. You left me with too much life to fuck up and I hate you.

A few weeks later I walked up to the hospital for my appointment with Dr X., my stomach creeping, remembrance latching me. I knew I would be held silent and must hear the evasion sidle past my blockaded urgency.

Fear still held me, no longer a human being, but something that could be pulled here and there, yet something that might still make trouble, whose story could make black difficulties.

Ten years before, in the dust of reference libraries and bookshops, I had found what I wanted, absorbed it, filtered it, hustled my thoughts, written notes, scrutinised them and reread them over a sandwich on the Green.

The information had seemed arcanely to funnel into my mind, books almost falling into my hands, toppling from the shelves, presenting themselves, insisting, begging my attention, the knowledge drawn into me from other lives and certain deaths. Some of it I slotted into my memory, ready for playing back when I needed to check it, and some I asked my daughter to type for me.

Thus, under my belt was first Section 127 (1 and 2) of

the Mental Health Act with details of prison sentences for sexual offences with patients. Second: The National Health Act, scrupulous in theory at least.

And more engrossing than either of these was 'Law Relating to Medical Practice' with its suggestion of unswerving decency in both vocations.

I had spent weeks uncovering new sources, sometimes with significant results. I had learned, for instance, that to caulk the shifting tidal menopause with shock may compel a queasy haunting, day and night for life. And I discovered a condition known as 'Survivor Syndrome', a complex of guilt, despair and anger, to be found in animals and humans, both of which have been known to die of its consequences, of which stress-related disorders are a great part. For me one of these was a stigmatic rash that wept and burned in the centre of my palms for some weeks, heralding future disorders.

I was much helped by having vertigo and incontinence, the side-effects of the tranquillisers I had been prescribed.

In boxes and envelopes I had copies of the fourth-century Hippocratic Oath, quotations from Hermes Trismegistus, the Aquarian Gospel, the French and English versions of Pascal's Mystic Amulette and, joining the spill of reference books in a baker's basket: *The Encyclopaedia of Numbers*. Loved, valued, and guiltily stolen from a library.

Perhaps I thought I was going to write something with the help of such spillikins of knowledge as I had assembled on the kitchen table. But I knew that however sweetly you withdraw one for scrutiny, the rest may jar, stir, unsettle, dislodge and all fall down.

I was the falling down of a pattern, I was the statistics of it. I didn't need to read it, but I did. I read that divorce was frequently the outcome of sexual offence and so was suicide. Though catharsis would have helped, I understood. And if I could not win this stealthy battle that had turned me dupe for so many years, still I could fight my own ill-fatedness.

Using my experience, common sense and instinct, I demolished Dr X.'s interpretation of psychiatry, delivered some enlightenment upon ethics and upon the needs of his patients and pointed out that the first step to therapy was communication, without which nothing could be achieved.

I looked at him in the silence that followed, and thought, I bet none of your poor fucking patients have ever spoken to you like that before, and let's hope I'm not the last to do it.

Rejoicing, I went downstairs to wait for a taxi. I hadn't fluffed, and I hadn't dried, but I was shaking, because since that first hospital I had always shaken easily.

But I felt good. Sixty years of mental notes were docketed in my mind, ready to be played back in my head whenever I wanted, and cradle-to-grave recall purled through my memory. Moreover, my little legal blood, whilst not indispensable, would keep my mind and perceptions sharp despite shock treatment and drug-thuggery.

The cab driver said: 'Been visiting someone there?'

I said: 'No, I *am* someone.'

He said: 'Looks like a nice place.'

I said: 'It's an institution. If you know what I mean. The only difference is the plastic flowers.'

He said: 'I get you. Everything got up to look posh and you pay double.'

And double for saving other people's skins, I

thought. Dead leaves railed against my ankles as I got out of the car. A lit sky and the autumn term. The house was empty and agreeable, and I smoked my last cigarette, keeping the empty packet for security. Lapsang soothed, and there was a wodge of loose-leaf paper on the kitchen table. I drew a map on it and a sea monster.

Doors had begun to open on to sheeted casualties and honourable fear that I had deserted in that place, some neither patients nor mental, but flawed human beings unable to speak or write their hatred and despair. Some were left there because their embarrassing handicaps might rupture Christmas, some because they were merely old. One had dared to be a midget. It was not worth keeping such people silent. No one would have believed them anyway. They were off-cuts.

The place has been rebuilt as bright as a penny, people tell me. Bright as a penny.

But even on handsome days that belong as much to other people as to me, that sound comes out of me, like a destitute.

I sat at the table and thought of my siblings' vapourings, sharp with fear that my madness might graze their charted lives. Their letters were spattered with exclamation marks like fits of coughing.

On a sheet of paper I drew a great knife, swagged and swagged again with blood. Hatred and fear were sealed in me by the urgent guilt of the medical profession, and thus garrisoned I fought a tongue-tied battle, raw and clammy. When they ignored me I exulted at their ineptness, when they shouted at me I marked the exact words in my memory and took victories for mine.

But if this battle were lost to them and I locked in

silence still, who would exhume the truth? Other victims perhaps, for I had been the patsy since 1969 when this body of respected men and women had first deodorised and buried the viscid truth. Thus, mute as mortality, fear lay across my hope eclipsing any spunkiness I falsely showed, and fear stays with me in surgeries, consulting rooms and the mental hospitals that bundled me out of the way to make certain of my silence.

I fought only a seeming power, a street bully, a seedy thug, pallid with anxiety for his reputation. But I am not brave. I am not, and it took courage to consider a stab at hypnotherapy which could offer a pleasant and a gentle anodyne. I might even be allowed to talk, a catharsis steadfastly refused by the Doctors X. and Y., for if I had talked, my words might edge into other consciences and higher authority, and endeavours to make a victim accept the crime are in my view corruptive and may have a more serious effect upon the unfortunate than the original wrong-doing, particularly if that took place in a hospital.

I knew I must leave the reeking battle and go softly towards my life's salvation, and softly hush my guarded hopes, and then perhaps as softly my knots might slip undone. I prayed for it, and passionately read about Dr Mesmer, but hypnotherapy had not a murmurous sound – rather it was angular and Greek-ish and my stomach still crept and wandered. Yet the rough edges of my mind began to knit up, and nursery fears were dandled. I felt a kick of hope inside me, as brave and furious as a baby's. I had felt that kick when I went to Turin to see the Holy Shroud.

I was full of anger and old reasonable sadness. Boy-o, you shouldn't have left me to mind the shop for God's sake. I turned on a frail axis, circle for circle and thread against thread, until I was counter to each revolution and wept most days.

Take away my thoughts, take my memory, you bastard, next of dead, my best of kin. I didn't want to feel my centre check out that awkward bright day.

I felt a kind of death when you said that giving me up was the only unselfish thing you'd ever done, but didn't say anything because the balance of my mind was seriously disturbed. The white plates were very pretty.

The balance of my mind stuttered when the newspapers said you had killed yourself, and the coffee spilled.

After that, my life ran counter to any rhythm that might be expected by other people or other prison sentences, twisting and burning like a snake round a staff. Mistakes filled the gaps I would not acknowledge, and were pushed beneath consulting-room carpets. Each gale of madness began with a storm of writing, plugged by tablets in case I disturbed the sensibilities of others by exposing my own.

My dear, dear boy, so untidily dead and still so much a belonging of mine. For years and beyond them I have been beleaguered by memory when I had thought myself free, and even now I am full of anger and old reasonable sadness.

But I'm still here. And my mind, my brain, my judgement, taste and capacity for pain are mine.

That night I went to bed and did not sleep for fear of a fresh nightmare – that the ordeal awaiting me next day might see me hypnotised into a pillar of salt and unable to put the washing in the machine. My stomach had dragged when I picked up the telephone and wrote in my diary: Thursday, November 18th – Hypnotherapy,

John Smith, and I was deadly nervous when I arrived, for though I felt armed, there was a meagreness of spirit in me as I rang his bell. My mouth dried out.

When the door opened, it was a little grig of a man that stood there, so jauncy, a cricket, a bright little twig, with a handlebar moustache and a Fair Isle pullover. The day was brilliant, sharp and cold as I said, 'Mr Smith?' and it was, and my hope thickened a little with relief.

Two hummocky cats sat on the stairs. 'Fred', said Mr Smith, 'and Wilhelmina.' Half-closed citrine eyes. The hedonistic pleasure of resilient ears and dense conclusive tails, the sudden cupped paw. I respect the yeas and nays of cats and did not sport with them.

He led me into a biggish, tidyish pleasant indeterminate room, with a big desk, chairs, a divan, books, a usual room and good for thinking in.

I sat, he sat. Yes, I could smoke, he said. I took my shoes off, I believe.

Mr Smith knew what I was there for and was patient, but my speech was crippled to start with, forced and clumsy until suddenly, I think I can, Mr Smith, I can. And for about two hours I did a bloodletting and I was allowed it, was watched and listened to, without him writing anything down, my sprawling words taken and salted away in his mind. Now, five years later, he remembers how I looked, sat, what I said and could not say.

On that morning I talked, and my throat and eyes burned from the long time no–cry, no–talk, no–listen. But I felt in me the continence born of faith in a human being, almost as though its firmness turned and took me. I told him I felt dirty and that I felt shame, that I had allowed my life to be chopped away into a fear made lasting by other people's guilt. I said these things again, in a sudden scarlet fury – that I felt shame and weakness, and that I felt dirty, and was not able to value myself. I said such people were wicked, the word sounding simple and dark, and childish to me, and I told him of the nightmares that had bludgeoned me for so many years.

I said these things because I needed to, but sometimes felt a drawing back inside me – that I might perhaps be laughed at or disbelieved. But I was not. Mr Smith watched me and watched me, and I swallowed up his absolute listening.

No wonder Doctor X. and Doctor Y. had discouraged me from hypnotherapy. It looked as though a good deal had already been revealed. One day, I thought, I will shit on them. Several times. And I lit another cigarette and looked at Mr Smith, and we sat and said nothing, but went on looking at each other. With a difference, I believe.

The packeted voices of the psychiatrists who had felled my bravery for so long swam away from me, for he spoke a strapping language, honourable and sound and with a kind of innocence. What he said verified everything I knew from experience, but I needed to hear it.

He said that undoubtedly the severe shock and distress caused by such offences were enough to do great damage, while the actual extent of the offence mattered less than the mental and emotional impact on the victim. And he finished by saying that the temperament and background of the victim, whether male or female, were crucial and must always be taken into account.

Out of habit, feelings of revulsion still hacked at my guts, but a wing in me flapped. I felt drained, light, a little sick, different, weak, yet cherished. And it was a wonderful sensation, like returning to my own skin, familiar, close and safe.

He could not exorcise the memories completely, but could at least help me live with them, he said, and to start with put me under light hypnosis. Unfamiliar, not sedative, alleviating, it eased the flinching of me, giving me back the muscle I had lost. The knot had loosened.

I made another appointment, had no more than a word with the cats, said goodbye, and went out through the front garden that was noisy with creepers and shrubs, autumn-heavy and the sky a chancer. Dark, vulnerable figs in a greengrocer's, the desperate pink maw of a newborn inside them. I bought one, and when I got home, took it fairly on the kitchen table, yet softly and with joy. For I will always be a strong swimmer.

So, happier Christmas, Easter, summer-day talking. Olympian and magnanimous, the cats half accept me, and sit in the room like teapots until I spill them out through the door, leaving me to John's voice, heard without listening. I will never be entirely free of that remembered fear, he says. I understand, and cannot hope for the bullyboy shove of birth to expel it. But gradually a jigsaw of memories rearranged in my mind, which, since they were not unpleasant, bade them welcome. And there was someone to listen to my thinking, and who did not fill silences.

I had done with the drugs that had halved my wholeness, tied my tongue and clubbed the fight out of me for so many years. Still sometimes in dreams I trafficked in small sexual cruelties for my corruptors.

But once, coming out of sleep, I remembered walking barefoot up Jermyn Street in the dark, someone with me. In Floris's window fine sponges were set out, as